How To Day Trade
Forex
For Profit

Harvey Walsh

SHELFLESS

How To Day Trade Forex For Profit
Published by Shelfless Ltd.
Copyright © 20012-2013 Harvey Walsh
All rights reserved.

First Edition (1.3) published 2012, revised 2013
ISBN 978-1490561868

Risk Disclosure Statement

Day trading has large potential rewards, and also large potential risk. You must be aware of the risks and be willing to accept them in order to invest in foreign exchange markets. Do not trade with money that you cannot afford to lose. The content of this book is for general information purposes only. Although every attempt has been made to assure accuracy, we assume no responsibility for errors or omissions. Examples are provided for illustrative purposes and should not be construed as investment advice or strategy. Hypothetical or simulated performance results have certain inherent limitations; unlike an actual performance record, simulated results do not represent actual trading. Also, since the trades have not actually been executed, the results may have under or over compensated for the impact, if any, of certain market factors, such as lack of liquidity. Past performance is not indicative of future results.

Contents

Foreword

When I was young I used to enjoy playing the board game Othello (sometimes called Reversi). It involved little plastic discs, black on one side, white on the other. The game was perfectly described by its tagline: *A minute to learn, a lifetime to master.* That tagline always stuck in my mind, and I often think of it when trading, because it almost perfectly describes that activity too.

Trading is simple to learn. The basics can be grasped easily in a weekend. Trading *profitably* can be very hard though. The simplicity of the theory is deceptive, almost a hindrance. When something is easy to learn we expect it to be easy to do, and are quickly disappointed if we cannot quickly perform as well as we would like. This disconnect between expectation and reality accounts for a great chunk of the people who decide they will trade, and who subsequently give up because they find they cannot make money. There are lots of other reasons traders fail, but I believe this to be one of most common.

In this book, I am not trying to suggest that you can "get rich quick" from trading forex. I'm not even going to suggest you can get rich at all. It takes more than a book to do that. It requires application and dedication. What this book *can* do is put you on the right path. Setting off in the right direction with the right basic knowledge should at the very least ensure that you don't end up getting *poor* quick, which is unnervingly easy to do with forex.

For some reason I have yet to fathom, many books and courses on trading fail to cover the essential groundwork. Maybe that's because would-be traders are keen to get to the money stuff, the juicy charts and trade setups that promise to make them thousands of Dollars overnight. Unfortunately without a solid grasp of the basics, those charts and setups are worthless (or worse; trading badly doesn't just fail to make money, it loses it). I believe the key to consistent profitable trading is to understand *price*. Price is like a language. It communicates to you, and if you understand it, it will guide you to good and profitable decisions. You can get by without speaking price, just as you can go on holiday to China without speaking any Chinese. But you'll have a far more rich and fulfilling (not to say easier) experience if you speak the lingo. Learn to speak price, and you will have a skill that you can use to make money for as long as there are markets to trade.

How To Use This Book

I have to admit I usually dislike it when books include a *How To Use This Book* section. You've paid for the book, you should be able to use it however you want, whether that be as the author intended, or as novelty gift wrap. However, there is logic to the way this book has been structured, so here are some guidelines on how you may want to use it to get the most out of it.

First, I urge you to try and avoid skipping chapters, even if you've read other books on trading. The information here is presented in order. Missing out chapters regardless of whether or not you are already familiar with the subject, may cause confusion later when I refer back. Even if you already understand the concepts and are just reading this for some specific setups, going over the initial chapters is good revision and will remind you why the setups work the way they do.

Second, I've included a number of *Missions* throughout the book. These are your homework, things to do when you're not reading. Taking on the Missions will greatly increase your chance of success. They will also make the transition from "reading about" trading to "doing" trading that much easier, because you will already have got your feet wet as you go through the material.

Third, in the text you will find some words are in *italics* when they are first introduced. You can find definitions for these terms in the Glossary at the end of the book.

Finally, there is a *Resources* page on this book's website, with links to useful stuff mentioned herein. Products and services come and go, and websites change their links on a whim. So rather than embedding links in the text only for them to stop working a week later, the Resources page remains up-to-date. You can find the Resources page at www.daytradingfreedom.com/forex-resources.

Introduction

Why Trade?

People get into trading for all sorts of reasons. For some it is about the freedom. Certainly that was the motivation for me. Working a nine to five, answering to the man, all in order to fill the coffers of some faceless enterprise was not my idea of fun. I wouldn't go as far as to compare a day job to prison, but you can probably see why I might be tempted.

For others, trading for a living is all about the purity of the activity. Most methods of earning an income involve providing some kind of service. Making stuff, selling stuff, moving stuff, writing stuff, installing stuff, building stuff, all of it involves transactions between the person doing the job and the person getting the service, often via an intermediary (like an employer). Stuff gets done, and payment is made in return. Trading isn't like that. No service is provided to anyone, at least not in any sense we would recognise. Buying and selling happens, and if there's a profit at the end, we get to keep it. Trading disconnects the effort of doing something from the income gained by doing it. For a given amount of work, there is no predetermined income. It may be that while lots of income is derived one day, another day income could be lost for the same amount of effort.

More importantly, a trader is solely and uniquely responsible for making their own living. There is no dependence on an employer to sign a pay check, and no dependence on a customer to pay for goods or services. If the trader fails to make money, they only have them self to blame. On the flip side, if the trader does very well, they have the satisfaction of knowing that it was entirely down to their own efforts.

Some trade just because they love it. There is no doubt there can be great joy to be had from analysing a market, deciphering a chart, making a prediction, and then watching it get fulfilled in real time.

And for some people, trading is not about the freedom, or the purity, or the inherent joy of the activity itself. It is simply about the money. These are the people who find trading the most difficult. Doing anything just for the payout can be soul destroying. There needs to be more motivation, otherwise trading is just a job like any other. There is no freedom or enjoyment from doing something because it has to be done. Trading profitably is simple but not easy, there are many hurdles to overcome. If you are trading because you want to, you will have less trouble jumping those hurdles.

Why Day Trade?

Time for a quick definition. A day trade is any trade which is opened and closed on the same day. If you buy something in the morning and sell it again in the afternoon, you made a day trade and henceforth can call yourself a day trader. Day trading is a very particular form of trading. Many will tell you that it cannot be done profitably, or that it is only for seasoned professionals with years of experience. This is, I am glad to say, nonsense. Day trading is accessible to all, and as long as it is approached sensibly, nobody need lose their shirt.

In fact, I would argue that day trading is safer than trading in other time frames. True day trading means not holding any position open overnight, ever. Everything bought during the day, must be sold off before the end of the same day. This offers the day trader the not inconsiderable advantage of knowing that should anything happen during the night that adversely affects the price of whatever they are trading, they will not be losing any money. They may lose the *opportunity* to *make* money from any such overnight price change, but that is not the same as waking up and finding one's trading account wiped out because the price move was in the wrong direction. Day traders sleep better!

Another advantage day traders enjoy is the freedom to take time off from the trading screen whenever they want. Traders holding positions open over days or weeks must check in on those positions daily, managing them, nursing them. Day traders close up their computer at the end of the day and have no trades open, no exposure to the market, and no need to open the computer again until the motivation strikes to trade for another day. Personally I tend to trade just three or four days a week. The rest of the time I don't have to switch a computer on. I don't need to plan vacations or trips away around WiFi access in order to keep an eye on my trading account. I don't need to sneak out of a restaurant between courses to check that my positions haven't taken a loss. I'm only trading when I'm actually trading.

As if the lack of overnight risk and the freedom from constantly checking trades wasn't reason enough to day trade, here's another—smaller trading account balances. Day traders are looking to take several small trades each day, all adding up to good size profits. Because these trades are small, it is only necessary to risk very small amounts of capital on each one. That in turn means the day trader's account can be operated with a lower initial balance. Day trading can be done on a smaller budget than longer term trading. So much for being just for major players with bags of experience and deep pockets!

Why Forex?

Of everything out there to trade, why choose forex? Why not stocks, bonds, futures, or commodities? Certainly all of those *instruments* have their own advantages and disadvantages, and indeed I am a great advocate of trading stocks myself. But forex has a number of unique advantages that make it a good choice, particularly for the beginner trader.

The biggest of these is that it is extremely cheap to get started. Most forex brokers offer free price charts to their customers. Accounts can be funded for a few hundred Dollars, sometimes under a hundred. With charts included, and online order entry systems provided for you, there are effectively no start up costs, assuming that you already have a suitable computer and internet connection. This low barrier to entry makes forex a popular choice among novices. Just because it attracts traders with little or no experience though, doesn't mean it is the easiest market to trade—it's not. For my money, US stocks provide the simplest and most profitable trades, but the cost of getting started is considerably higher. Forex might not be *as* easy, but as you'll learn in this book, it's not difficult either.

Another great benefit to trading foreign exchange is that it is available 24 hours a day during the week. Wherever you live in the world, whatever timezone, if you want to trade at two o'clock in the morning, well, you can. Now although the market is open all hours, that is not to say that there are good trades to be had any time you want—there aren't. Certain periods of the day and night provide richer pickings than others. There are enough of these hot spots spread throughout each 24 hours that even if you have a day job, you can reasonably expect to be able to day trade forex in the evening after work.

A third feature of forex, and one often touted as a great advantage, is its high leverage, or gearing. We'll dive deeper into that particular subject later on, for now suffice it to say that the higher the gearing, the more money you can effectively risk with each trade. Forex is geared so highly that you can trade with $100 and make it seem like you are trading with $10,000 or more. This is great, it means you have the potential to make the kind of profits you could make if you really were trading with $10,000, but just with your little $100 account. A nice advantage for sure, and one that makes it possible to see returns in the hundreds of percent per day. There is a downside though, and a pretty big one. Gearing is a double edged sword. Just as you have the potential for huge profits, so you have the potential to make massive losses, far greater than your initial $100 deposit. In fact there is almost no theoretical limit to how much you can lose, although in reality your broker will cut you off long before things get too dire. The main thing to understand at this point is that forex has the potential for you to lose far more than just your initial stake, it's not like betting on the horses.

The fourth big benefit currency trading has to offer is its relative lack of regulation. Normally we think of regulation as being a good thing, the kind of thing that stops people building airports in our back gardens, or banks taking massive risks that end up bankrupting entire economies (clearly regulation doesn't always work!) When it comes to day trading, regulation can make our lives more difficult. Rules about minimum account sizes, asset classes, and short selling all get in the way of actually placing a trade. The forex market is largely unencumbered by all of that. You can set up a free account on a forex broker's website, load up some funds with a credit card or PayPal account, and off you go. Again, this is a double edged sword. Starting out without knowing what you are doing is a direct route to the poor house. Fortunately you're not going to have that problem, as you are in possession of this book.

The fifth and final reason forex is a great market to trade is its very technical nature. As we'll see later on, we can learn to read the market through technical means, a bit like reading a formula. Although we'll be concentrating on day trading, the technical trades we'll be making can work on much longer timescales than just day trades. In other words, once we know how to make a trade that lasts a few hours, we can make the same type of trade but have it span days or even weeks if that's what we want. We can move from day trading to swing trading without having to learn different or additional skills. The forex market itself is flexible and works well across these different time frames. An added benefit is that many of the skills you will learn in this book, because they are based on these technical criteria, can easily be transferred to other markets like stocks or futures. Learning to trade forex is a great way to get into trading almost anything else.

Chapter One

How We Trade Forex

Making money from forex is relatively straightforward. It's the same basic idea as making money from the stock market, but instead of buying and selling stocks, we buy and sell currencies. We buy one currency with another, hoping to later sell that currency back at a higher price, profiting from the difference. We'll be delving into how all this works in a lot more detail as we go along, but before we start there is some basic terminology and some concepts we must cover. Don't worry if these don't all make perfect sense straight off, each will be covered in greater depth when the time comes. For now, we just need to make sure we have an idea of the essentials.

Every forex trade involves two currencies, the *base* currency, and the *quote* currency. We use the base currency to *buy* the quote currency, and we *sell* the quote currency for the base currency. Here's an example forex quote:

EUR/USD	
1.31	1.31
06	**08**
SELL 2	BUY

Let's break this down into its components. At the top of the quote is the name of the currency pair we are looking at trading. In this case, that pair is EUR/USD which is shorthand for Euro / US Dollar. Currency pairs are always written in this format, named using the ISO 4217 codes for the currency names. These standard codes are three letters and each denotes a specific currency. EUR is the code for the Euro, USD for the US Dollar, GBP for British Pounds Sterling, AUD for the Australian Dollar, and so on. For a complete list see the link on the Resources page.

The first currency in the pair name is the base currency, so in this example that is the Euro (EUR). The second currency is the quote currency, here that's the US Dollar (USD). Some websites or brokers leave out the slash ("/") between the two currencies, but the order is always the same.

If we wanted to trade this example pair, we would buy US Dollars with Euros. It's pretty much like going into a shop and buying bread with Dollars. We would walk out of the shop with some bread, and fewer Dollars in our pocket. In the case of our forex trade, we walk away with some US Dollars, and are lighter by a number of Euros.

When it comes to sell our Dollars, we would be paid for them in Euros. If the price of the US Dollar had increased in relation to the Euro, we would make a profit.

The *price* of the quote currency (the US Dollar in this example) is the number shown in the boxes on our quote. In fact there are two numbers shown, the one on the left is marked *Sell* and the one on the right *Buy*. If we want to *buy* the quote currency, it will be at the right hand price. This is called the *ask* price, because that's what is being asked for the currency being sold. Here the ask price is 1.3108, which means one US Dollar will cost us 1.3108 Euros.

The *sell* price on the left is the price we can sell our US Dollars for. This is also know as the *bid* price, because we are bid that amount for our US Dollars. Here the bid price is 1.3106, so we can sell one US Dollar for 1.3106 Euros. The difference between the bid price and the ask price is called the *spread,* which in this case is 0.0002, or two *pips*. A pip is effectively one ten—thousandth of a unit of currency (the fourth decimal place). It is usually the smallest amount the price of a currency can change in a forex quote. In the case of the US Dollar, that means a pip is one ten—thousandth of a Dollar, or one hundredth of a cent.

If we were to trade this EUR/USD currency pair, here's how things might happen:

Step 1: We buy ten thousand US Dollars. The ask price is 1.3108, so ten thousand US Dollars is going to cost us 13,108 Euros.

Step 2: If nothing changes, and if we decided to sell our US Dollars back, we would do so at the bid price which is 1.3106. That means we would get back 13,106 Euros, making a loss of 2 Euros on the trade.

Step 3: The price of the US Dollar increases relative to the Euro. The ask price moves up to 1.3138 and the bid price moves up to 1.3136. That means the price has risen by 0.0030, which is thirty thousandths of a Dollar, or 30 pips.

Step 4: We sell back our ten thousand US Dollars, getting back 13,136 Euros, which is 28 Euros more than we paid at the start. Therefore we have realised a profit of 28 Euros.

The price moved 30 pips, but because of the 2 pip spread between the bid price and the ask price, we actually made 28 pips profit. The 28 Euros profit worked out at 1 Euro for every pip that the price changed. We bought and sold ten thousand Dollars. If we had bought and sold one hundred thousand Dollars, we would have made 10 Euros per pip profit, or 280 Euros, from exactly the same trade. Forex then, offers us the possibility to *scale* our trades and make substantial profits even from very small changes in the price of currencies.

Don't worry if this makes it sound like you're going to need to be a millionaire to trade forex, as we will see later on we don't need to spend thousands of Euros or Dollars on trades in order to make good profits.

Short Selling

We don't have to wait for prices to rise to be able to profit from forex, we can do so when they fall too. There are two ways we can achieve this. The first is simply to flip the quote and base currencies. If we believed the US Dollar was going to *fall* in value against the Euro, then instead of buying US Dollars with Euros (i.e. trading EUR/USD) we could buy Euros with US Dollars—that is—trade USD/EUR. If the value of the US Dollar fell against the Euro, that would be the same as saying the value of the Euro had increased against the US Dollar. We could then sell back our Euros for more Dollars than we paid for them, making a profit.

Flipping pairs like that is one way to profit from falling prices, but it does have disadvantages. One is that not all brokers offer currency pairs in both directions. Another is that it can become confusing if we are buying and selling the same pair, but flipping the direction of that pair between trades. Fortunately there is another option which overcomes both these shortcomings and makes life much easier. That option is *short selling*. In short selling (often just called *shorting*) we can sell something we don't yet own, get credited with the proceeds of the sale, then buy it back again at a (hopefully) lower price and pocket the difference. Selling what we don't own is mercifully very easy in the world of forex, because our broker will lend it to us. If, for example, we were still trading the EUR/USD pair and believed that the value of the US Dollar was going to fall in relation to the Euro, here is how our trade might happen:

Step 1: We sell ten thousand US Dollars. The bid price is 1.3106, so our account is credited with 13,106 Euros from the proceeds of this sale. Because we didn't actually have any US Dollars to sell, our broker lent them to us. We are now said to be *short* 10,000 US Dollars.

Step 2: The price of the US Dollar falls agains the Euro. The bid price drops to 1.3056 and the ask price drops to 1.3058. The price has fallen by 0.0050, or fifty pips.

Step 3: We buy back ten thousand US Dollars at the new ask price of 1.3058, costing us 13,058 Euros. The Dollars go straight back to the broker who lent them to us. We are no longer in debt to anyone, and after buying back the Dollars we still have 48 Euros left over from the sale in Step 1 (13,108 Euros credit from the sale - 13,058 Euros spent to repurchase them). Our profit was 48 Euros from this 50 pip price drop (remember there was always a 2 pip spread between the bid and ask prices, which is why we didn't make 50 Dollars profit).

Although it sounds like there's a bit more involved in short selling, in practice the process is exactly the same as regular "buy first" trades. The whole business with the broker lending us currency to sell happens in the background, we don't see it. As far as we are concerned, we just need to figure out if we think the price of the quote currency is going to rise or fall relative to the base currency, then buy or sell accordingly.

How To Profit Trading Forex

Clearly, figuring out if currency prices are going to rise or fall is pretty essential to the whole business of trading forex. Much of this book will look at ways of *trying* to do that, but the unfortunate fact of the matter is that nobody in the world knows for sure at any given time, where currency prices are heading next. We can make an educated guess, and the more educated the better, but we are never going to get it right one hundred percent of the time. The good news is that we don't need to. We can be wrong about price changes and still make money. In trading, being wrong is okay. Indeed I encourage you to positively embrace being wrong. It is as much a part of the job as being right, but psychologically that can be hard to get to grips with, which is why it is worth starting to get your head round the idea right now.

There are three ways we can be profitable by trading forex and being wrong. Our first possibility is to try and be right more often than we are wrong. If we make ten trades, for seven of them we correctly predict the direction the price moves and for the other three we are incorrect, we should end up making a profit overall. Our second possibility is to make bigger profits when we are right than we make losses when we are wrong. If we taken ten trades and are right about price direction only three times, and wrong seven times, we could still be profitable overall. If each of the three winning trades make a profit of $100, and each of the losing trades makes a loss of $20, then we are quids in. Three winners x $100 = $300 in winnings. Seven losers x $20 = $140 in losses. Subtract that $140 from our $300 winnings and we still have $160 profit left over. The third possibility, and this is the one to aim for, is to combine the other two—try and be right more often than we are wrong, *and* at the same time make bigger profits on our winning trades than losses on our losing ones. Combining those previous two examples, if we are right for seven trades taking $100 profit on each, our winnings are $700. If we lose $20 on each of the three losing trades, that's a total loss of $60. After the ten trades, we end up with a net profit of $700 - $60 = $640.

Given that we don't need to be correct in our prediction about future currency prices all the time in order to be profitable, it must be true that when we want to trade we could just flip a coin, going long (buying) if it lands heads up, and going short (selling) if it lands tails up. Such a *system* can be profitable, more so than some far more complex systems actually, but we can do a lot better than that. We can use clues handed to us by the price itself to make an intelligent prediction about the most likely future direction of that price, and trade accordingly. Doing so will increase our rate of hitting winners. Later in the book we will build a trading system—a method for choosing when to take trades, in what direction to take them, and when to exit them. Our system will use the clues handed to us by the price. We will try and be right more often than we are wrong, and when we are right we will maximise our profits. When we are wrong, we will keep our losses to a minimum.

Being right about the direction of price more often than we are wrong about it, is a little harder in forex than some other markets, because forex is a slower moving market (presenting fewer trading opportunities) and a less predictable one than, say, some stock markets. On the plus side, when we are right about price direction in forex, it is usually possible to let our trade run on a long time, taking good profits from a single trade. Faster moving markets may offer more trades per day, but each of those trades tend to be over much more quickly. In forex, we lose frequency but gain in profitability per trade. Forex is also much easier to scale than many other markets, meaning once we have a system that works, we can increase the amount of money we risk on each trade, and proportionally the amount of profit made per trade. And as a final bonus, most forex brokers these days offer trading without charging commissions (they make their money in other ways, as we'll see).

Our Objectives

As we dive into the world of forex and examine it from every angle, deconstructing it and analysing what makes it tick, it will help if we can keep in mind our overall objective. It's pretty simple, to make money right? And the way we do that is to take consistently profitable trades. And the way we do *that* is to constantly figure out where the price is headed next, try and be right about that more often than we are wrong, and to maximise our winnings on those occasions we are right, minimising them when we are wrong. This bears repeating as it's so important to have in the backs of our minds as we go forwards. Our goal in everything we do in the forex world is simply this:

• Use the clues the price gives us to constantly have a view on where we think it is going next.

• Use that view to buy and sell currency pairs to try and profit from those price changes.

• When we are right, make the most of it.

• When we are wrong, recognise it and get out of our trade with the minimum loss possible.

Our goal is *not* to make blockbuster trades netting thousands of Dollars profit every day. It is not necessarily even to make profitable trades every day. Some days, those trades simply aren't there. The markets can be slow, not much happens, and there is simply no opportunity to take a trade with a decent level of probability of success. Recognising when not to trade is every bit as important as recognising when we should trade. We don't risk our money in the market just for the sake of it, that would be reckless. We cannot force the market to give us profits every day. The days where nothing happens are more than made up for by days when things move wildly. But most days will be average, and that's just fine. We don't need stellar trades every day to make a lot of money. We saw in our earlier example a trade where the price moved 30 pips. Accounting for the spread, that trade made 28 Euros profit. By scaling up, that could easily have been 280 Euros profit, or 280 US Dollars (for the sake of simplicity). One trade like that each day would net $1,400 profit per week, or about $5,600 per month, or about $61,000 per year. I don't know about you, but to me $61,000 a year profit for one trade per day sounds like a good return on my time.

What if we scaled things up again, and doubled the money we put down on each trade? Without changing anything in our trading strategy, without doing any extra work, we would suddenly have the potential to make over $120,000 a year, all from one trade a day. That is why small consistent wins are the key to success in forex. Sure, it's great to read stories on forums or blogs from traders who had an amazing day, making thousands from a couple of trades. But what about all the days when they lost hundreds? Slow and steady wins every time.

Now we know what we are trying to achieve, let's dive in and start to unravel the world of currencies, markets, brokers, and trading.

Chapter Two

Understanding Currency

A thorough understanding of what money is and how the foreign exchange market works, is essential if we are to have any hope of profiting from it. If we truly understand the intricacies of what makes the value of currencies change, we have a much greater chance of making short term predictions about what those changes are likely to be. As forex traders, our job is to make such predictions in order that we may buy and sell currencies and profit from them. So let's see just what is going on with these currencies. The first step in understanding them, is understanding what money is. Sounds kind of obvious, but is it?

Most countries use what is known as a *fiat* money system. This has nothing to do with quirky Italian cars (although the origins of the word and the brand name are undoubtedly the same, being a Latin word meaning "let it be done"). Fiat money is simply money that in and of itself has no intrinsic value. An American ten Dollar bill for example, is not worth ten Dollars because the paper that it is made from and the ink printed upon it combine to a value of ten Dollars. It is worth ten Dollars solely because that's what the US government says it is worth. The same goes for a ten Euro bill, a ten Pound note, and so on.

It wasn't always like this. Prior to 1971, the US Dollar was directly linked to the value of gold. Although a ten Dollar bill still wasn't physically worth ten Dollars, it could—in theory at least—be exchanged for ten Dollars worth of gold (in fact, between 1944 and 1971 the value of US Dollars was fixed at thirty five Dollars to one troy ounce of gold.) So money had a fixed value. In 1971 though, President Nixon ended this relationship between currency and gold, and the US Dollar became a fiat currency. Now ten Dollars was worth, well, ten Dollars! Because other so-called *reserve* currencies are linked to the Dollar, they also lost their direct link to the value of gold.

Put another way, prior to 1971, the value of currency was directly linked to the value of gold. As there is a finite amount of gold in the world, by implication there was a finite amount of currency available. In 1971 that link was broken. The amount of currency that could potentially exist became infinite. At the same time, the possible value of currency also became infinite. Ten Dollars could be worth nothing at all, or it could be worth enough to buy all the gold in the world. Its value depended entirely on perception. Whatever the consensus view of its value was, that was its value.

It may sound strange, but that's how all currency works today. Governments can, and do, literally create money out of thin air. Banks do this all the time. Any time anyone takes out a loan from the bank, the bank is indirectly creating additional currency from nowhere. It's not the purpose of this book to go deeper into how that process works, but if you are interested in finding out more, check the Resources page on the book website for a link to some videos which explain in more detail. The point is that the value of any currency is simply what people perceive it to be. No more, no less.

The fact that perceptions of value are constantly changing is what makes forex trading possible. Today, the consensus view might be that one US Dollar is worth 0.75 Euros. Tomorrow, that consensus may well have changed, and the view could be that a single US Dollar is worth 0.76 Euros. The "price" of the Euro would have changed. Any situation where prices are changing is a situation that can be traded and profited from. Equally of course, such situations can also lead to losing money.

If you've followed along so far, there should be a glaringly obvious question by now. Who or what decides what any given currency is worth? That question is at the heart of the foreign exchange market. The simple answer is that the people who hold the currency are those who decide what it is worth, and that includes the likes of you and me. But it's a bit more complicated than that.

The Island of WahWah

To understand how currency is valued we are going to examine an imaginary microcosm of the finance world. Let us imagine a little island, isolated in a huge ocean, oblivious to the existence of the rest of the world. We'll call this island WahWah, for no particular reason. On the island of WahWah live two tribes, we'll call them the Smiths and the Jones. The Smiths live on one side of the island, a land rich in minerals and iron ore. They have learnt how to extract this ore, melt it down, and purify it. In other words, the Smiths are able to produce metal.

On the other side of WahWah the Jones do not have any of those mineral deposits. However, their territory is richly forested. There are an abundance of different types of tree, and thick lush vegetation. The Jones have become experts in felling wood using rudimentary stone tools. They can work the wood, producing all sorts of useful things from shelters to spears for catching fish.

The islanders, like any society, have figured out that different people are good at doing different things. For instance, the man who makes the spears is rubbish at making chairs. So if he needs a new chair, he trades a few spears for a nice comfy seat from the woman who is good at making those.

The Smiths and the Jones know of each others existence, and being peaceful people, are happy to extend this system of bartering between the two tribes. By huge coincidence, both tribes came up with the same calendar system used in the western world. Every Saturday morning, residents from both sides of the island meet at a spot in neutral territory on a hill in the middle. The Smiths bring metal implements, blades for cutting wood, knives for cutting food, that kind of thing. The Jones bring an array of wood based goods, like chairs for sitting, and forks for eating. Knives are exchanged for forks, chairs for blades, and so forth. At the end of the morning, each tribe goes home happy. It's an efficient *market*. Each tribe has a finite amount of raw resource, so the value of the goods are easily determined.

The Creation of Currency

Fast forward a few generations and things have moved on economically on WahWah. The Jones tribesmen and women have got a bit fed up with having to carry around chairs and knives every time they want to go shopping for a simple loaf of bread or a pint of milk. It's inconvenient, and frankly the baker already has more chairs than he knows what to do with. Not only that, but a chair is worth about five loaves of bread. If the chair maker only wants one loaf, they're a bit stuck. How do you trade a fifth of a chair?

The tribal elders have pondered the problem, and come up with a new system. They've issued everyone with a bunch of paper notes. Each note has a fixed value, it is worth one tenth of a tree. The tribal elders know how many trees there are in the forest, so they know how many paper notes they can issue. Since the tribesman have been dealing in wood based products all their lives, they know that if a paper note is worth one tenth of a tree, then it must also be worth one loaf of bread (because one tree is worth ten loaves of bread), or one pint of milk, or half a knife, or one fifth of a chair. Now the Jones can carry around a pocketful of these convenient paper notes instead of logs or wooden products. When they want some bread, they trade a paper note for it. Then the baker can use some of those notes to buy milk, or whatever else he needs, instead of amassing rooms full of chairs. All the tribesmen and women know that at any time they can exchange ten of their paper notes for a tree from the elders, and so the value of these notes is easily and universally understood. Everyone agrees it's a pretty awesome system, especially the women who invent a new pass time, recreational shopping.

Through the jungle grapevine, word of the Jones new system reaches the Smiths. They think this is a great idea, and immediately implement the same thing within their tribe. They issue paper notes which are valued based on one ingot of metal. Ten notes are worth one ingot. Because everyone knows what they can trade an ingot of metal for, so everyone knows how much one of their new paper notes is worth. As long as the number of paper notes in the village doesn't exceed ten times the number of ingots, the value of the paper notes is a fixed and known quantity, and the system holds up.

Trade Routes

Now when the Saturday inter-tribe market comes round, both the Smiths and the Jones bring their fancy new paper notes as well as their regular goods. This is where problems arise. To a Jones tribesman, a Smith paper note has no value. Nobody back on the Jones side of the island is going to accept this strange note! So when a Smith offers to buy a chair with five of his Smith notes, the Jones chair maker refuses the deal. The same thing happens in reverse. No self respecting Smith is going to accept a Jones note for one of his valuable hand crafted knives.

Clearly something has to be done. The elders of both tribes get together to sort out a solution. These elders, being powerful people, happen to have retained large reserves of their respective tribes' paper notes. As a service to enable efficient trade between the tribes, they agree to trades notes between themselves.

Now when market day comes around, things are a little different. A young woman from the Jones side of the island requires some metal for a new project she's working on (a prototype car, and although nobody has invented the wheel yet, that doesn't appear to be curbing her enthusiasm for the idea). She requires a whole bunch of metal panels. The Smith who sells metal panels understandably wants to be paid in Smith notes. So miss Jones go to the Smith tribal elder and exchanges fifty of her Jones notes for fifty of his Smith notes. Now she can use her newly acquired Smith notes to buy the metal panels. The panel-selling Smith is happy, he can take the Smith notes he's just been paid and use them to buy anything he wants back home.

As it happens, a certain Mr Smith is working on an idea for a wheel. He doesn't know what he'll do with it yet, but he's pretty fired up about the whole thing. He needs some logs from the Jones, thinking perhaps if he slices them up, they might be just what he's looking for. He goes to the Jones tribal elder and exchanges twenty of his Smith notes for twenty of the elder's Jones notes. Now he can go to the log selling Jones and buy a couple of logs with his Jones notes. Log-seller Jones is twenty Jones notes better off, and he takes these back to spend in his favourite beachside bar.

At the end of the market day, everyone is happy once again, they all got what they wanted. The number of Smith notes and Jones notes in circulation hasn't changed, thus neither has their value.

After a few weeks of this, tribal elder Smith has almost no Smith notes left, but he does have a lot of Jones notes. Tribal elder Jones is in a similar position. They get together and swap over a few hundred Smith notes for a few hundred Jones notes. Now each is once again rich in his own *currency*, and efficient trade between the tribes can continue.

Decoupling

Fast forward another few generations. Things are really motoring now, almost literally. Miss Jones of prototype car fame, met and married Mr Smith the inventor of the wheel. The resulting vehicles that have sprung forth from this marriage have become a big hit on both sides of the island, and really opened up travel between the two villages.

Economically too, things have changed. To fuel this great revolution on the island, both tribes required more Smith notes and Jones notes. To try and meet this need, the Jones began planting more trees, and the Smiths were mining metals like crazy. But they weren't producing raw materials quickly enough to satisfy the demand for more paper notes. So they took a bold step. The elders started making more notes than there were raw materials to back them.

On the face of it, a Jones note was still worth one tenth of a tree. But as there were now more than ten times as many notes as trees, that value was only nominal. It had become theoretically possible for someone to amass enough notes to buy all of the forest, and still have some notes left over. If that happened, what would those notes be worth? If there was no longer any guarantee that a note could be exchanged for actual wood, what was its real value? Within the village, this wasn't too much of a problem. Everyone had been using the notes all their lives, and their value was something that was taken for granted. Nobody consciously made the link between a note and a fixed quantity of wood in the forest.

Exactly the same thing was happening over in the Smith village. Smith notes had become decoupled from metal ingots, and their value was also something that was just assumed within the village.

Unfortunately this gave rise to a new problem. The actual paper notes themselves cost virtually nothing to make. With the cost of production almost zero, each village could potentially make as many notes as they felt like. That meant, for example, that the Smiths could turn up at the market on Saturday with thousands of Smith notes that they had made overnight (at no cost), and buy all the Jones notes from the Jones elders. The Jones could do the same thing. If this happened, each village would be flooded with thousands of notes causing their perceived value to simply evaporate. The economy would grind to a halt. Clearly, something had to be done.

Foreign Exchange Is Born

The tribal elders once again got together to look for a solution to this looming problem, and being clever chaps they found one. They built a giant set of weighing scales. These they installed on a plinth at the top of the hill in the middle of the island, where they could clearly be seen from everywhere in the market. One side was labelled with a giant J, and the other side with a giant S. Every Saturday morning before the market opened, the Jones elders deposited their entire stock of Jones notes on the J side of the scale, and the Smith elders placed all their Smith notes on the S side. As the scales settled, everyone around could see the quantity of Jones notes *relative* to Smith notes. From this, the elders could calculate the value of a single Smith note relative to a single Jones note, in other words, the *exchange rate*. With this rate fixed, fair and balanced trade could take place in the market. If, during the week, the Jones created more new notes than the Smiths, their side of the scales would weigh down more heavily, and so the value of a single Jones note relative to a single Smith note, would drop. The exchange rate for that week's market would have changed.

The system was clearly a bit cumbersome, and relied on a lot of trust on each side, but being only a metaphor for the world economy, each village was happy to live with it.

The Exchange Rate

The weighing scales on the island of WahWah are of course an oversimplification of how currency exchange works. Nonetheless, they serve as a good basis for understanding the matter, so we'll continue to use the metaphor. Let's look in more detail at how the exchange rate on WahWah was calculated, and its implications for trade.

On a particular Saturday at the start of summer, the number of Jones notes on the J side of the scale is exactly the same as the number of Smith notes on the S side. For the sake of simplicity, we'll imagine there are 100,000 notes on each side of the scale. There is one Smith note for every Jones note (100,000 divided by 100,000 = 1). Therefore one Smith note is equal in value to one Jones note. The *exchange rate* is 1 to 1.

A Smith villager decides to buy 100 Jones notes. He hands over 100 of his Smith notes to a Jones elder, who removes 100 Jones notes from the scale and hands them to the Smith villager. The exchange is carried out at the rate of 1 to 1. What happens to the scales? The Jones side is now 100 notes lighter, and so lifts ever so slightly. 100 notes from a balance of 100,000 is tiny, and the movement in the scales is almost imperceptible. But if 99 more Smith villagers carry out the same transaction, each purchasing 100 Jones notes, things start to happen. By the time the last villager has purchased his Jones notes, the Jones side of the scale is looking a lot lighter. 100 Smith villagers each bought 100 Jones notes (100 x 100 = 10,000). The day started with 100,000 Jones notes on the scale, and ended with just 90,000. Jones notes haven't exactly become more scarce, there are as many in circulation as before, but there are fewer available for trade from the elders.

Again for the sake of simplicity, we'll assume that no Jones villagers bought any Smith notes, and therefore the Smith side of the scale remained at 100,000 notes. What does this do to the exchange rate? There are now 100,000 Smith notes on the scale for

90,000 Jones notes. 100,000 divided by 90,000 is 1.11, in other words there are 1.11 Smith notes for every 1 Jones note. The exchange rate has changed to 1.11 to 1. All other things being equal, Jones notes are now a rarer commodity than Smith notes. Their value relative to Smith notes has increased. It is reasonable to expect the Smiths to now pay 1.11 of their Smith notes for every 1 Jones note. This is great news for the Jones villagers. Turning the exchange rate round the other way, we can see that the Jones/Smith rate is 0.9 to 1 (90,000 Jones notes divided by 100,000 Smith notes). So they now only need pay 0.9 of their Jones notes to buy 1 Smith note. This makes products sold in the Smith village effectively 10% cheaper for the Jones! Not such good news for the Smiths though, as Jones notes have become more expensive, making products purchased from the Jones more expensive.

If during the week, the Jones elders decide to make a bunch of new Jones notes, two things will happen. Inside the Jones village, the value of the Jones notes will become diluted. If there are more notes around, each note is effectively worth less. To combat this problem, the villagers who sell stuff just put their prices up to compensate (*inflation*). The other thing that happens is that these new notes will be added to the Jones side of the scales at the next market day, causing it to tip downwards again. The value of the Jones notes relative to the Smith notes will drop. The Jones will lose some of the buying power they gained the previous week by the rise in value of their notes.

The system of scales helps keep the fledgeling economies of both sides of the island in check, by discouraging the creation of new paper notes.

Speculative Trading

Things carry on this way for a while, with the exchange rate being calculated on the massive scales every Saturday morning. As the trade between the Smiths and the Jones ebbs and flows in each direction, so the rate goes up and down. Some weeks it favours the Smiths, other weeks it favours the Jones. The elders continue to trade notes between themselves, keeping currency in circulation. They use the same exchange rate as fixed by the scales, carrying out their private trade at the end of market day each week.

One particularly enterprising young Smith has been watching the exchange rate for some months, and has realised there is profit to be made. He's figured out that every time there is a big storm on WahWah, the wooden houses that all the islanders live in tend to get a bit battered, and many need repairs. The Smiths, having limited wood reserves of their own, are obliged to buy more wood from the Jones on market day, so that they can repair their homes. Inevitably that means they must buy more Jones notes with which to purchase this wood. Equally inevitably, that means the Jones side of the weighing scale is going to get a lot lighter, raising the value of Jones notes.

Our young Mr Smith, sensing opportunity, takes to studying some basic meteorology. Within a few more weeks, he's become pretty adept at predicting the arrival of these battering storms. It turns out storms on WahWah come round like clockwork (quite why nobody else realised this remains unknown). He's worked out that there's a new storm likely in just over a week. Come Saturday, he buys 1000 Jones notes. As luck would have it, the exchange rate that day is 1 to 1, which makes this example nice and easy to follow. He spends 1000 of his Smith notes, and walks away from the market with 1000 Jones notes, and a big smile.

Wednesday arrives, and brings the storm with it. It's a big one, and hits the Smiths side of the island head on. Lots of wood shelters lose their roofs. Plenty of repairs need to be carried out. On Saturday at the market, thousands of Jones notes are bought by Smiths, who then spend them on wood. The Jones side of the scale tips up considerably as it becomes lighter and lighter. The following week when the exchange rate is calculated, it turns out there is now one and a half Smith notes for every Jones note. The exchange rate is 1.5 to 1. That makes the cost of a Jones note 1.5 Smith notes. The cost of a Smith note is just 0.66 Jones notes, or put another way, 1 Jones note now buys 1.5 Smith notes.

Our hero takes his 1000 Jones notes purchased two weeks earlier, and uses them to buy back 1,500 Smith notes. He hasn't done any work, and no new notes have been created, but by correctly predicting the change in the exchange rate, he is now 500 Smith notes better off than a couple of weeks ago.

News of this apparently magical method for acquiring notes spreads like wildfire, and soon all the villagers from both sides of the island are at it. Speculation about all sorts of things becomes rife. Is there any truth in the rumour the Smiths are running out of metal? What about the news that half the Jones have been struck down with a mystery illness and can't make any new chairs or forks? Hard news and idle gossip alike are analysed and reanalysed, as the villagers speculatively buy and sell each others notes, trying to profit from the exchange rate. The market becomes so busy it opens every day instead of just Saturday. The exchange rate fluctuates so wildly, it is calculated every hour instead of just at the start of the day. Then every half hour, and eventually, in real time for every transaction.

What's Wrong With WahWah

The islanders of WahWah now have an almost fully functioning economy, with two currencies, and a thriving foreign exchange market. But as a model for the real world, there are problems. For one thing, the system assumes the exchange rate is based only on currency held by the tribal elders, it doesn't take into account all the rest of the money in circulation. When the Smiths buy all those Jones notes, they use them to buy wood—from the Jones. So the Jones notes actually end up back on the Jones side of the island. The Jones also have the Smith notes that were exchanged for their own notes, so the wealth has been transferred to their side of the island. The Jones are wealthier than the Smiths, so their currency is worth more. Although the scales do show this, they don't fully disclose all the reasons for it, they show only the relative scarcity of Jones notes.

Another problem is that although the elders on WahWah represent banks, they don't yet issue credit to their villagers. Credit is the single biggest means by which new money is created, so it has a huge impact on the value of currency.

Despite these limitations, the idea of a giant set of scales representing currency available to trade is still a useful metaphor, and we'll continue to use it in this book. As long as we understand that the scales aren't a literal representation of the exchange rate, we can use them as a nice visual way to think about the value of one currency relative to another.

WahWah vs The World

WahWah represents a nice simple model of foreign exchange. The real world is more complex, not least because there are an awful lot more "tribes" than just the Smiths and the Jones. Most countries have their own unique currency, and they can all be traded with each other. We can buy US Dollars with British Pounds Sterling, or with Euros, or Australian Dollars, or just about any other currency. Likewise we can buy Euros with Pounds, US or Australian Dollars, Japanese Yen, etc.

Rather than there being one set of scales calculating the exchange rate, every country has numerous sets, each loaded up with a different currency on the opposite side. To make matters more complicated, these scales are all interlinked. If the value of the US Dollar changes, it must change relative to all other currencies, otherwise an opportunity for *arbitrage* would occur (don't worry if you don't know what arbitrage is, we're going to discover in just a moment). This is an important point, and deserves closer investigation.

Interlinked Currencies

Let's look at three major currencies, the US Dollar, the British Pound Sterling, and the Euro. At a given moment, the exchange rates are as follows:

$1 = £0.64
£1 = €1.2
€0.76 = $1

If we took ten US Dollars and exchanged them for Pounds, then exchanged those Pounds for Euros, and those Euros for US Dollars, leaving aside any commission costs, we would reasonably assume that we would end up back with the ten Dollars we started with. Here's how that calculation would look:

First we exchange ten US Dollars for British Pounds: $10.00 = £6.40
Now we take our 6.4 Pounds and buy Euros with them: £6.40 = €7.60
We complete the triangle by purchasing US Dollars with our Euros: €7.60 = $10.00

Everything works out, and we end up with the same ten Dollars we started with.

What would happen if the exchange rate between the US Dollar and the British Pound changed, for example to $1 = £0.70, but the Pound Sterling to Euro rate and the Euro to US Dollar rate both remained unchanged? Let's do the calculation again using the new rate:

First we exchange ten US Dollars for British Pounds: $10.00 = £7.00
Now we take our 7.0 Pounds and buy Euros with them: £7.00 = €8.40
We complete the triangle buy purchasing US Dollars with ourEuros: €8.40 = $11.00

By simply changing ten US Dollars into Pounds, those Pounds into Euros, and then those Euros back into US Dollars, we end up with $1 more than we started with! Clearly this is an untenable situation, as anyone with any sense will immediately make those transactions with much larger amounts, netting guaranteed profit for no risk, and potentially harming the value of the currencies in the process. The situation represents a short term anomaly, and profiting from anomalies like this is called *arbitrage*.

Actually these kinds of anomalies can and do occur every day, but they are tiny— thousandths of a Dollar or less, and they only happen for microseconds at a time. Some market participants can and do make arbitrage trades to profit from these situations, but those very trades are what close up the anomalies and cause all the inter-linked sets of scales to right themselves. (We'll look more at who the market participants are later on.)

To us mere mortals though, the takeaway message here is that a change in the value of one currency has a ripple effect, causing changes in the values of all other currencies as they relate to each other. It's an important point to bear in mind as we explore in more detail what makes the value of currencies change.

What Is Price?

As we've seen from the island of WahWah and our real world example, foreign exchange trading is all about trying to profit from the changing values of one currency against another. As forex traders we're going to need a way to figure out when and how those values are going to change, so we can—like the enterprising Mr Smith—be in a position to profit. In order to have a fighting chance of doing that, it will help if we understand more about what makes these currency values change.

The value of anything that can be bought and sold can be measured by its *price*. A transaction takes place when one party values what the other party has, more than they value what they can offer in return. For example, back on WahWah the Smiths have an abundance of knives, more than they could possibly use themselves. The Jones are in a similar position with regard to forks. For a Smith, the fork being offered by Mr Jones is worth more to him than the knife he could exchange it for. The reverse is also true. Mr Jones sees more value in the knife of Mr Smith than the fork he currently has. A deal is done, knife and fork are exchanged, and both parties are happy. They both got value from the transaction. The value of one fork was equal to one knife. We could say that the *price* of a fork is a knife (and vice versa).

When money comes along in the form of new fangled paper notes, the same concept still applies. Mr Smith and Mr Jones still have their knives and forks, and they also have a pocket full of paper notes. Mr Smith needs another fork. The paper notes in his pocket can be used to buy anything on WahWah, but right now he needs the fork more than anything else. So he is happy to exchange money for the fork. And Mr Jones is happy because he needs money more than he needs another fork. The transaction is the same, the value of the fork is just being measured against some money instead of against another object. The *price* of the fork is now the money that Mr Smith paid.

When you go shopping, or pay rent, or your electric bill, or indeed buy anything else, the same thing is happening. You need a roof over your head, and food in your belly, more than you need the money you are using to pay for them. The price you pay for any of these things is arrived at by mutual agreement between you and the person selling it to you. You may well want to pay less for your loaf of bread, but the baker values their bread as being worth a certain amount of money. If you think that price is too high, you don't hand over the money and you don't get the bread. The transaction only occurs when both parties get what they want.

Now, if *nobody* buys the baker's bread at the price he asks, he will eventually end up with a lot of stale bread that he can do nothing with, and he won't have any money. The value of the bread relative to money is diminishing as the bread ages. Sooner or later he has to drop the price until the people with the money agree that the value proposition is correct, and they hand over some money for the bread. The buyers will have moved the price of the bread.

So as we can see, *price* is nothing more than the *perceived value* of something *relative to money*. It is arrived at by mutual agreement of the parties on either side of the transaction. This is an absolutely key concept in trading. When we trade we are trying to determine future prices in order that we may profit from the difference between the price now and that future price. Understanding what price actually represents is essential to understanding how and why it changes.

The price of currency is no different to anything else that can be bought or sold. We can buy one currency with another. One currency is the commodity being sold (the *quote* currency in the pair), the other is the money being used to purchase it (the *base* currency in the pair). Which is which really depends on your point of view. Either way, the *price* of money is simply its value in relation to other (different) money.

What Moves Prices

We've already seen how basic supply and demand can cause prices to change. When the baker finds no demand for his bread, he is forced to lower the price until it matches what the market is willing to pay. But there are other factors that feed into the price equation. For example, what would happen if there were two bakers in town, but one closed down due to retirement? With no competition around, the remaining baker could raise his prices and the market would—up to a point—have to bear it. At some point, the market would decide it was a better deal to drive to the next town, and thus the maximum price of local bread would be found.

There are other ways the baker could change his prices. For instance, he could increase the size of his loaves, giving more value. Conversely, he may decide to lower his prices, thinking that doing so would stimulate demand. He may sell more loaves at a lower profit per loaf, but make more money by selling higher volume.

Whatever the baker does with his product and the price he asks for it, he is never really in full control of that price. The buyer is the ultimate arbiter of price, he can always walk away from the deal. From the buyer's point of view, it's all about *their perception* of value.

Certain aspects of the deal cannot be argued with. All other things being equal, a 900g loaf of bread should command a higher price than a 600g loaf. The weight of the bread is an attribute that is easily measured and valued. But what about the quality of the bread? Two bakers may both be selling 900g loaves, but what if one tastes better? A better flavour should command a higher price, yet the attribute of *flavour* is something that is down to the perception of the buyer.

Then there is the bakery itself. Bakery A might be clean, welcoming, and have convenient parking just outside. Bakery B might be a bit run down, staffed by grumpy bakers, and be difficult to get to. Which can charge the higher price? What if the bread from bakery B is far tastier than the bread from bakery A? Now which can charge the higher price? Only the buyers of bread—the *market*—can truly decide. Their perception of which is the better deal will determine the prices each bakery can charge.

Investment Prices

So much for pricing a commodity like bread, what about pricing investments? After all, we're looking at figuring out price changes of currency because as day traders we are buying and selling it for the sole purpose of trying to make a profit. Well, the same model applies to investments, but buyer perception plays an even bigger role, particularly perception about *future value*.

Let's take real estate as a quick example, it's something most people can easily relate to. An investor looking for a house to rent out and maybe sell on for a profit in the future is going to have to ask themselves three types of question about any house they look at. Firstly, they will look at certain easily measurable and easily valued attributes. Is the house big or small? How many bedrooms are there? What about bathrooms? Is it immediately habitable? Does it have all mains services connected (water, electricity etc). These are bare minimum attributes that most people can agree on and put a value to.

Next come the more perception based attributes. Is the big garden a plus point (easier to rent to families with kids) or a negative point (more expensive to maintain)? What about the fact it is located on a busy road? Maybe that's a good thing (easy to get to, quick to get into town) or maybe it's bad (noisy, dirty, dangerous). The way the investor sees the answers to these questions will have a direct bearing on their perceived value of the house.

The final layer is the perception of future value, after all, this is an investment so the objective is for it to increase in value over time. Is the area the house is located in good or bad? If it's bad now, is it "up and coming" and expected to improve over the next few years? If it's good, will it remain good, or is there a new high speed rail line about to cut through the back yard? Will there be more houses built here soon? If so, will those make the area more desirable by bringing in new people, or will they cause an over supply of housing, pushing the value of existing housing stock down?

The answers to these three layers of questions will determine the value of the house to any given buyer, thus the price *they* are willing to pay. Furthermore, if the majority of investors looking at the house have a similar perception about its value, more of those investors will be potential buyers. That would mean there is increased demand for the house, which in turn will likely push up its price. So once again we see that the buyers hold all the power when it comes to setting price, whether it be the price of bread, or of an investment property.

What Moves Currency Prices

Let's recap quickly before moving on to look at currency prices. We've seen that the price of any commodity can be set by a seller, but is ultimately determined by potential buyers' perception of value. In the case of investments, perception of future value is an additional factor.

So what about the price of currency? Money is both a commodity and an investment. If you need money to spend while on vacation, or to buy something that can only be paid for in a particular currency, then that money is a commodity. You are not concerned with its future value, only what it is going to cost you right now.

On the other hand if you are buying currency with a view to reselling it at a profit, then that's an investment and the decision is all about future value. As forex traders, clearly we fall into the latter category. Here's where currency transactions differ from regular investment transactions. In a normal deal, such as our real estate example, the seller of the real estate is exchanging property for money. The buyer will be looking at the potential future value of the property, but the seller will be looking at the immediate value of the money. In other words, the transaction is a commodity (money) in exchange for an investment (the real estate).

When we make a foreign exchange deal, we're looking at money on both sides of the deal. The transaction can be viewed as a commodity (money) for another commodity (different money). Or it can be seen as a commodity (money) for an investment (different money), or most likely, as one investment (money) for another investment (different money)! In this last example, each party is both buyer and seller. Both are interested in the potential future value of what the other has to offer. If I buy some Euros and pay for them in US Dollars, and I do this as an investment, that suggests I believe the value of the Euros I am buying is going to go up relative to the Dollars I am selling. Likewise, the person on the other side of the deal presumably believes that the value of the US Dollars they will be acquiring from me will appreciate in relation to the Euros they will be parting with. Only one of us can be right (although both of us could still profit from the transaction).

All of this means that pricing currency is a more complex affair than pricing other commodities. The buyer has all the power in setting a price (no transaction can occur until a buyer is happy with the price), but when trading currencies, both parties are buyers and sellers in equal measure. Fundamentally though, the same process occurs as in any other sale. Buyers and sellers on opposite sides of the table will figure out what they think a fair price is, based on their own perception of the future value, and when they can agree, the deal is done. We'll look into the mechanics of how this works in the forex market later on. Before we do though, we need to look in some detail at the elements that go into building up that all important perception of future value.

Price Perception

As forex traders, our job is to get a "good" price both when buying and selling. Given our objective is to buy currency at one price and sell it at a better price, profiting from the difference, a large part of our job is to form an opinion of what the future price is going to be.

There are two ways we can do that. One way is to look at prices from the past, spot repeating patterns, and use those to determine when are good times to buy and sell. This is called *technical analysis*, and we'll be delving into that in another chapter.

The other way is to look at all the factors that can and will affect the perceived value of the currency we are interested in trading. Remember, if the majority of participants in the market believe that the price is going to rise, that fact alone will cause the price to rise. Studying these factors, or fundamentals, is called *fundamental analysis*. When we come to design our trading strategy, we'll be using some fundamental analysis mixed with some technical analysis, so a good grasp of both is essential.

The Players

If the price of currency is determined by the future value as perceived by the majority of participants in the market, it would be useful to know who this majority actually are. Who are these people studying currency? Why are they doing so? What is their interest in the price and the possible future price? Knowing the answer to these questions will go a long way to help us get an idea of what the market as a whole is thinking. In the world of forex, here are the main players:

Governments

It almost goes without saying that Governments are the biggest spenders in the world. Any organisation charged with collecting and spending billions of Dollars worth of money, clearly has an interest in the future value of that money. Whilst tax is collected in the local currency, a portion of government spending occurs in the world at large and therefore numerous currencies are involved. Vast sums of money are spent on defence, healthcare, education, and civil projects. If Australia decides to buy some new air defence jets from the US for a few billion US Dollars, small changes in the US / Australian Dollar exchange rate can alter the cost of the deal by millions.

Governments don't just spend, they borrow too, a lot! Some borrowing comes from banks, a great deal also happens by issuing bonds (a sort of private fixed interest deal). To anyone buying a bond, the value of the currency that bond is issued in will be very important. Someone from Germany buying a UK government bond valued in Pounds Sterling is going to want to know that those Pounds will be worth something by the time the bond matures and they get their money back. So governments need to protect the value of their own currency in order to secure their borrowing power.

It might appear from this that every government wishes their currency to be valued highly relative to other currencies. After all, that makes for cheap borrowing and cheap purchasing of foreign goods. But a high currency price is a double edged sword. It makes home grown goods more expensive to foreign buyers. The UK may enjoy cheaper borrowing if the Pound remains highly priced relative to, say, the Euro. But for anyone in Europe, that makes British goods seem expensive. For example, if the French aircraft company Dassault wanted to purchase some British Rolls Royce jet engines, a high Pound relative to the Euro may be enough to put them off. That means no sale for Rolls Royce, which in turn means lower tax payments to the UK government. Governments then, have a vested in interest in keeping their own currency price stable relative to other currencies.

Central Banks

The Federal Reserve, the Bank of England, the European Central Bank, every country (or currency block) has a central bank, also known as a reserve bank. Their precise roles and powers differ slightly from country to country, but generally speaking they exist to try and maintain the stability of their own currency, both in relation to others (by influencing exchange rates) and internally (by trying to limit inflation). Central banks also usually regulate the banking industry within their country. Although some of the largest central banks (including the Federal Reserve) are run independently of government, broadly speaking they work to meet government economic policy.

Of most interest to us as forex traders is the role of central banks in influencing exchange rates. There are a few ways they can try and do this. One such way is simply by participating in the foreign exchange market themselves. By buying and selling very large quantities of currency, they can effectively take money out of the market. They can also put money into the market by making more of it (adding more cash to their side of the giant weighing scales). Their other big weapon is interest rates. Changing the base interest rate within their own country makes it easier or harder to borrow money, which in turn may stimulate or slow the economy. A healthy economy usually means a strong currency, but too healthy could mean inflation, which can hurt currency values.

Investment and Retail Banks

Banks play a dual role within the currency market. On the one hand they act as a player in their own right, trading currency for the profit of the bank itself, and for the bank's clients. On the other hand, they act as a facilitator, granting access to the money market for their clients. We'll discover more about the facilitator role shortly when we see how we ourselves can participate in the forex market.

By far the largest proportion of the currency transactions which take place every day involve banks. Even plain old retail banking (i.e. managing current and savings accounts) is implicated in the market. If you live in the US, and Uncle Bob from Canada sends you a cheque in Canadian Dollars for your birthday, you can cash that cheque in your regular US bank account (in which case, no doubt you would refer to it as a "check"!) Your bank would credit you in US Dollars, calculating the value of the credit using the exchange rate in force. Behind the scenes though, they won't simply trade your Canadian Dollar cheque for US Dollars. The cheque will be cashed and the funds added to a Canadian Dollar denominated fund. The bank's own traders will then choose a time they believe to be most advantageous to carry out the transaction converting that money into US Dollars. That could be immediately, or it could well be in a few years! In fact, banks hold large reserves of most currencies, and trade them for other currencies in an effort to make profits from the fluctuations in exchange rates, just like we're going to do, although not on quite the same scale.

Brokers

If you have ever bought or sold stocks, you will be familiar with the role of brokers. They literally broker the deal between parties, those parties being you and the stock exchange where the deal is done. In the case of foreign exchange, there is no central exchange like the stock market. Instead, all transactions occur between market participants. Banks will deal with other banks, central banks will deal with with central banks and other banks, and governments with each other and with banks and central banks. That takes care of the bigger players, but what about the likes of you and me? If you wanted to sell some US Dollars for Euros, and I wanted to buy some Euros for US Dollars, we could do a deal. But it wouldn't be a very efficient way to carry on, looking for just the right person to deal with every time we wanted to exchange one currency for another. That's where brokers come in. They act as a middle man, holding funds in many currencies. You could sell your US Dollars to a broker who would pay you in Euros, and I could buy those US Dollars from the broker, paying for them in Euros. If you wanted to sell back your Euros for US Dollars, but I wasn't interested in doing another deal, that's no problem, the broker has a float of both currencies, and will happily do the deal with you.

Strictly speaking, "broker" isn't the right word. These private companies are effectively market makers. But throughout this book I will use the term broker because most people are familiar with it and understand the idea. For the likes of you and me, most of our forex trading is going to be done through a broker. A little later, we'll see how they make their money, and how they set the price you can buy and sell currencies at.

There are two basic kinds of broker in the forex market. One is the "bureau d'echange" type retail broker, the kind you find in airport lobbies and on high streets. They deal in cash, handing out spending money for your travels (usually at an exchange rate considerably more favourable to them than to you!)

The other type is the online trading broker, designed for the likes of us—people who are buying and selling currencies actively for the purpose of profit. These kinds of brokers won't be sending you bundles of foreign banknotes every time you do a deal. Instead, you'll deposit funds with them and trade with those funds, leaving them in their care.

Companies & Organisations

Any company that deals internationally, that is to say is involved in import and / or export, or has a presence in a country other than their own, has an interest in the currency market. If Uncle Bob in Canada has an award winning bakery, the chances are all of his transactions occur in Canadian Dollars. He buys his raw materials locally (flower, yeast, water) and sells his bread locally. If he gets an amazing deal on yeast from an American company, that company will likely want to be paid in US Dollars. Uncle Bob is now exposed to the currency market. If the value of the US Dollar falls, his yeast effectively gets cheaper. Uncle Bob's daughter decides to open a second bakery in London in the UK. The bakery is a wholly owned subsidiary of Uncle Bob's company. In London, ingredients are purchased in the local currency (Pounds Sterling), and the product is sold in the same currency. When it comes time to repatriate some of the profits back to the parent company in Canada, those Pounds will need to be exchange for Canadian Dollars. The rate at which that occurs could have a major impact on the bottom line of the company.

Clearly the bigger the organisation in global terms, the bigger the impact the currency markets have on their profitability. These kinds of currency transactions are carried out through banks.

Traders

The likes of you and me. We're interested in exchange rate movements purely for speculative purposes. We're in it to make money from the system. There's certainly nothing wrong with that, indeed we help add liquidity to the market by making sure there is always someone to take the other side of any currency transaction. We could trade through banks, but for our purposes, specialist brokers are far better adapted to our needs for reasons which will become clear.

What Is Everyone Looking At?

Now we know who all the interested parties are in the currency market, the next question is what are they looking at? If everyone is trying to figure out what the future value of a currency is, how are they doing it? Knowing this will help us in our own efforts to figure out where *we* think the price of currency is headed. After all, if the price is moved by the perception of the majority, we need to know how the majority are thinking. And to do that, we need to know what they are watching.

Government Policy

Governments, as we've seen already, are major players in moving currency prices. Each government has an interest in keeping its own currency relatively stable, but at the same time they have to get on with the job of running their country, and that means spending money. Where that money gets spent is going to have a big impact on the perceived value of their currency. Equally, where they get their spending money from is going to have an effect. So it is certainly going to be worth our while to keep an eye on major policy announcements. Things like:

Interest rates — Changing these can stimulate economies, bringing about more spending.

Budgets — The big three budgets for the government of any developed nation are defence, health, and education. Changes to any of these can spark more government borrowing and higher spending (often with foreign contractors). There can be other effects too. Cuts in defence budgets could leave smaller nations open to attack from less friendly neighbours. Increases in education budgets imply better very long term prospects (a better educated populace has higher earning power). The same goes for the health budget, a healthy population should be more productive, with all the knock on effects that go with it.

Taxation — All that spending money has to come from somewhere, and most comes from tax receipts. Higher tax means more spending money. But too high and it may force companies overseas, meaning less spending money. Sales taxes can affect imports and exports, which directly affects the quantity of currency entering and leaving the country.

Borrowing — The rest of a government's spending money comes from borrowing. Some of that is classic borrowing from banks. Some is from other nations. Who buys this debt, the repayment terms, and the interest rates, will all have an effect on currency price.

If at this point you are getting concerned that you're going to have to become an expert analyst on world politics and government policy, don't be. We don't have to understand the intricacies of how a policy change will ripple out throughout the currency markets. We simply need to be aware that it will. More importantly, we must understand that for the bigger players, those with the power to move prices, all of these kinds of policy are very important. If a G8 country doubles its defence budget, it's going to have an effect. Our job is just to be aware that that effect is about to make something happen. It is not our job to know what that something will be.

Statistics

Closely linked to government policy are official statistics. These are official audited numbers that give an idea about the health of a country's economy, a bit like taking its pulse. These statistics are released at regular intervals and predetermined times. All the players know when they are coming, and they always have an effect on currency prices as everyone tries to work out the implications. Again, for us as traders our job isn't to interpret any of these, we just need to know what they are, know when they are coming, and to understand that they are going to have an effect on the price of any currency we are trading. Here are some of the main statistics with the power to move currency prices:

Unemployment — A very clear indicator of the health of any economy.

House building — Healthy and wealthy economies build more homes.

Manufacturing — We tend to think of all manufacturing as having relocated to China, but that's not really true. Most G8 countries still count manufacturing as a huge proportion of their economy. Any changes in output can have a big knock on effect.

Trade Surplus / Deficit — A trade surplus means a country is exporting more than it is importing. All things being equal, that suggests there is more money coming into the country than there is going out.

Civil Unrest / War

Clearly any country that is experiencing any form of civil unrest is going to feel the effects financially. Unrest could be as minor as union strike action, or as major as all out civil war. Anything that affects the country's ability to do business as usual is going to be important.

War can have positive or negative effects. If the war is on home soil (i.e. the country in question is the one that has been invaded), clearly this is a bad thing in every sense. But a powerful country sending troops abroad? Well that can increase defence spending, which can mean jobs and manufacturing contracts, clean-up and rebuilding export deals, and so on. The effects are complex.

Credit Ratings

Just as you personally have a credit rating which takes into account your income, borrowing, and ability and willingness to meet repayments, so countries have credit ratings too. These are issued by ratings agencies like Standard & Poor, and Moody's. In effect, these agencies are constantly examining all the factors we have looked at above and more, and are working out for any given country, what all that means for their financial outlook. A healthy growing economy should mean a good credit rating. A country with a good credit rating will find it easier to borrow money. And a country that can borrow money can spend money, which means its currency should be healthy and strong. Any change in a country's credit rating will have immediate and profound effects on the price of its currency.

Happy Families

All this sounds like an awful lot of information to think about. Remember though, we're not trying to analyse every last detail, rather we are trying to figure out the general health of any given currency. Having a good idea of whether a particular currency is strong or strengthening, or weak or weakening, is going to be very useful when it comes to deciding if we want to buy or sell that currency. By maintaining an overview of all the factors we've just looked at, we'll have a good idea about the health of any given country's economy, and by implication the strength of its currency.

Thinking about whole countries might sound like it takes a lot of mental processing. But actually, countries are a lot like families, it's just that the numbers involved are bigger. Try to think of any country as being like a regular household with a mother and father and a couple of kids. In any household there is income and there are expenses.

Let's take an example. The Samson family income comes from the salary of Mr and Mrs Samson, both of whom work. This income is like tax revenue for a country. The Samsons have a vegetable plot in the garden, and solar panels on the roof. They sell the electricity these produce back to the grid, and they also sell some of their home grown fruit and veg at a local market, bringing in some extra cash. This cash is like income from exports.

The Samsons have plenty of expenses they need to cover. These include food and fuel. Some of their food comes from their vegetable plot, but much has to be bought from the supermarket (import). There is also household maintenance (civil projects), home security (defence), medical bills (healthcare), school books for the kids (education) and two cars to run (transport).

When it comes to borrowing, the family have a mortgage, and one of the cars is on finance. If the Samson family manage their income and expenses well, then they will keep everything in balance, and they may even be able to save a bit of cash each month. If on the other hand, they don't watch their spending, they will beed to put some of their purchases on credit cards, paying back later at high interest rates.

With some numbers to work with, if you knew Mr & Mrs Samson's salary, if you knew how much money their solar panels earned, and if you could see what they spent all of their money on, you could probably make a pretty good guess as to whether or not you felt safe lending them some money. You could even decide if you wanted to invest in them. Maybe you would see that they spend way too much, their credit card debt is mounting, and they're never going to be able to pay it off. If that were the case, you probably wouldn't want to risk your money with them.

What about if the family used their own unique currency? Would you feel safe swapping some of your regular currency for theirs? Would you be confident that you could sell it back at a later date and that it would be worth the same or more than you bought it for?

This is how we need to think of countries, like big families. The budgets are bigger, there are a lot more zeros on the numbers, but fundamentally their decisions about income, expenses, and investment have the same effect.

A Word About Europe

Europe is a bit more complicated. Seventeen countries from Europe use the same currency, the Euro. Whilst the European Union imposes certain targets on member states, economic policy is still locally managed within each state. It's a bit like having seventeen families living in the same apartment block, all using a big shared bank account. The apartment block owner sets out rules that say how much each family can borrow and spend, but ultimately those families manage their own finances. If one family overspends, it's going to have an effect on the others.

The uncertainly that comes from lack of cohesive financial policy in Europe is somewhat tempered by the stability of knowing that they can't let the whole system fail. Whatever happens, the member states have to work together to keep the everything running.

Currency Summary

Let's wrap up this section with a summary, and then we'll see why there's a lot less work involved in all of this than you might think.

The prices of currencies change relative to one another because perceptions about future values of those currencies are always changing.

Those perceptions are based on ideas about the health of the economies backing each currency, relative to other economies. These ideas can be garnered by looking at government policy, and economic statistics.

There are lots of parties with a vested interest in figuring out future changes in currency prices, and these include governments, corporations, banks, and individuals.

Some of these interested parties are obliged to exchange one currency for another at certain times, regardless of the exchange rate. For example, when importing or exporting goods.

Other parties exchange one currency for another purely speculatively, hoping to profit from changes in the exchange rate.

As traders, our aim is to try and predict short term changes in currency prices so that we may profit from them by selling one currency for another, then buying it back at a more favourable rate.

Now Let's Simplify Matters

All of this stuff is important, but there's too much information to take it all in and process it. We can't examine the economic policy of every country, just to try and predict where the price of its currency might be headed in the very short term.

Fortunately we can get round this in two ways. Firstly we can decide to specialise in just a few currencies. For example, we may decide to follow just the US Dollar, the Euro, and the British Pound. That would give us three ways to trade, buying and selling between each of those currencies. Remember though, all currencies are interlinked and even if we never intend to trade in Japanese Yen in our lives, another Fukushima style nuclear disaster in Japan will still affect our three currencies.

The second way we can simplify matters is by using *technical analysis* to summarise the past and give us clues about the future, and that's what we're going to look at next.

You might wonder why, if we can avoid looking at a lot of this stuff, I have spent the time explaining it. A reasonable question. The answer is that in forex as in any form of trading, the better you understand the market, the better you will understand the motivation of the people trading it, and the better your own trading will be. It's like learning to be a race car driver. Most people can drive a car without any clue as to what goes on under the bonnet, how the suspension works, or about the complexities of rubber tyre compounds. But at the level of professional racing driver, an understanding of all these things can help squeeze out a better performance on the track. Knowing how different rubber heats and cools enables a competent racing driver to take a corner at the highest speed their nerves will allow. Understanding how suspension works means they can adjust it to suit the track they are driving on. Knowing how fuel weight is distributed around the car, and how that distribution changes as the fuel is burnt, knowing how the wind direction changes air flow over the bodywork, knowing how the air temperature and ambient humidity affect the performance of the engine, all these things are in the mind of a driver as he pushes his machine to the limit. An experienced driver won't think consciously about these things most of the time, they will become second nature. But subconsciously, it's all there.

For us as forex traders it's the same. Anyone can walk into their local bank, plonk down a bundle of Dollars and ask for some Swiss Francs in exchange, and the bank will be happy to oblige. But the exchange rate will be considerably more favourable to the bank than the customer. And will that rate be looking so clever tomorrow? If the customer wants to become a professional trader, then they need to squeeze that rate to the maximum, and time their trade to the best of their ability. Understanding all the market dynamics we've looked at in this chapter will help. And just like for the racing driver, that understanding will quickly become second nature. As you develop as a trader, and as you continually observe the market and world economic conditions, you will acquire a real sense of how different news events shape the trading day, and that is something that can put you one step ahead in the game.

Chapter Three

Introduction To Technical Analysis

We can learn a lot from history, and the history of price is no exception. Prices tend to move in patterns that can and do repeat themselves. This applies to almost all prices, whether they be those of houses, gas, or of currency. Why do prices move in patterns? Because they are set by people, and people are creatures of habit. Technical analysis (TA) using price charts is the study of prices from the past in an effort to predict those in the future.

Patterns in prices occur both over the long term and the short term. Markets have a tendency to bubble over the long term, with prices rising until eventually they reach heights that are unsustainable. At that point the bubble bursts, prices fall dramatically, and there's a period of consolidation. This boom and bust bubble pattern occurs over the long term (years or even decades), and it is a pattern that has repeated itself over centuries.

Patterns occur over much shorter timescales as well. As we'll see, we can find the same kinds of patterns lasting months, weeks, days, hours, or even minutes. Why is that so? Again, because prices are made by people, and people have different outlooks — short term, long term, and everything in between.

There's another reason price patterns repeat, and that is because of *self fulfilling prophecy*. If enough people believe that when a price behaves in a certain way then it's going to do something or other, then those people may take trades according to that belief, and actually cause the price to do the "something or other" they were expecting. Self fulfilling prophecy is a very human trait. I have a friend who swears blind that every time it rains, he buys a lot of music. There is absolutely no logic to this link, presumably he just happened to have noticed it was raining once when he bought some music. Now that he believes it to be true, as soon as the sky clouds over, he's headed for the iTunes store. His belief in this mysterious cause and effect actually makes it come true.

Exactly the same thing happens with price patterns, although unlike my friend and his music fetish, there is already a link between the past behaviour of prices and their future movements, but the element of self fulfilling prophecy makes this even stronger.

Price Charts

Price charts are our main tool when it comes to TA. They are a graphical summary of the price of something over a fixed period of time. Anything that has a price can be charted. You could chart house prices, bread prices, prices in the iTunes music store, or as we will be doing, currency prices.

Price charts make it very easy to spot the kinds of patterns that occur in price movements. Consider this sequence of prices, then look at the chart of those prices:

1.29, 1.29, 1.30, 1.31, 1.32, 1.31
1.30, 1.29, 1.31, 1.32, 1.31, 1.29
1.31, 1.32, 1.32, 1.31, 1.3, 1.29

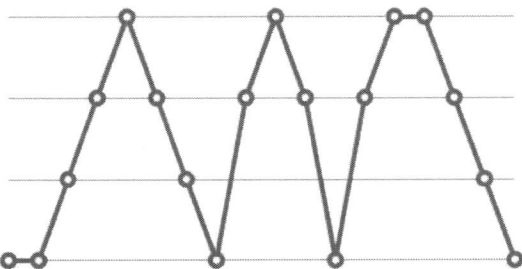

The repeating up / down pattern is quite easy to see just reading the numbers. But it's much easier to see in the chart. This is a simple example with a handful of prices. When we're looking back over more data, charts become invaluable.

Technical analysis is a very handy technique because we can learn it once and use it forever. If we based our trades purely on fundamentals (all those things we looked at in the previous chapter), we would need to spend a lot of time reading newspapers and reports. We would have to have our finger on the pulse all day every day just to keep up. Technical analysis doesn't entirely relieve us of the need to know what's going on fundamentally, but it does mean we can catch up with what's happened in the past at a quick glance.

Limitations of Technical Analysis

Technical analysis is a great tool, but as with any tool it is important to understand its limitations so we can use it for the purpose intended. A bread knife is a great tool for cutting bread, but you wouldn't try and chop a tree down with one, that would clearly be beyond its limits. A price chart is marvellous at telling you what has happened to the price of something up until now, but it cannot tell you why it happened like that, neither will it tell you what is going to happen next. Certainly it will give you clues, but they are only clues.

Sometimes charts can appear truly prophetic, with clear patterns signalling future price moves with uncanny accuracy. Just as often though, it can all go "wrong" because of some fundamental change—some bad or unexpected news.

Knowing these limitations means we can be prepared for them and act accordingly. If a chart is our main weapon as we walk into the market, then best we think of it has having a sticky trigger. Most of the time it's going to help us out, but sometimes it could be completely useless, or even blow up in our face. We should always have an escape plan for those occasions the chart fails us.

Anatomy Of A Price Chart

As the chart is our primary weapon, it will pay dividends to get to know it intimately. As traders, we will be spending a lot of time looking at charts, so let's dig in and examine how they work.

If you've ever looked at the chart of a currency price (or stock price, interest rate, or any other financial chart) in a newspaper or on the television news, it probably looked something like this:

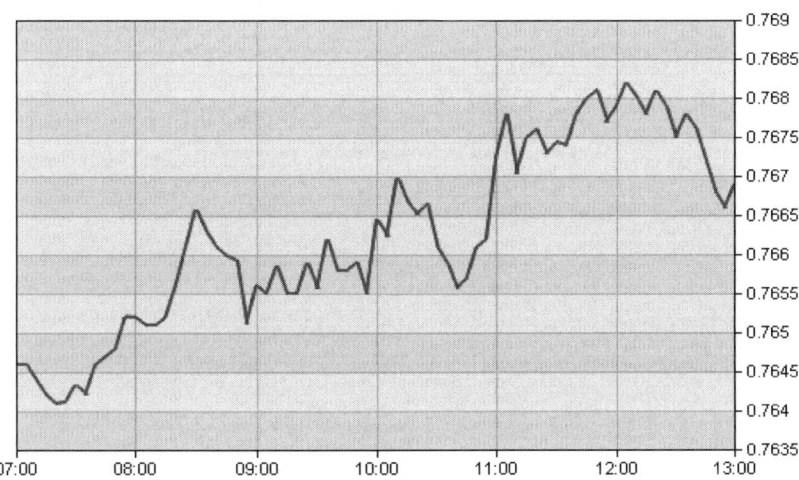

This chart, called a *line* chart, is pretty basic. Every forex chart compares two currencies, this one happens to be comparing the US Dollar (USD) against the Euro (EUR). The shorthand name, or symbol, for this currency pair then is USD/EUR. We always name currency pairs with the base currency first, here the US Dollar, and the currency we're comparing it to second, here that's the Euro. In other words, this USD/EUR chart is showing us how many Euros we can buy for 1 US Dollar. We could also look at this the other way round and say that the chart is showing us how many Euros a single US Dollar will cost us. At the very end of the chart then, we can see that 1 US Dollar could buy 0.767 of a Euro. Or to flip that round, you could buy one US Dollar with 0.767 of a Euro.

This simple chart shows us a high level overview of how the value of the Euro changed against the US Dollar during a six hour period. At a glance we can see that the Euro was getting slightly *weaker* against the Dollar. As the line goes up, it means we could buy more Euros with the same quantity of Dollars. And because we're looking at a pair of currencies, we can also see that the inverse is true, the chart is showing us that the US Dollar was getting *stronger* against the Euro—it cost more Euros to buy US Dollars.

If we think back to the giant weighing scales on WahWah, we could imagine this chart being drawn by those scales. We put US Dollars in the left hand side of the scales, and the right hand side we put in Euros. If we stuck a giant felt market to the left side of the scales, the chart above is what the marker would draw. As the islanders took Dollars out of the left side, that side would become lighter and lift up, causing the line made by the market to go higher. Remember, as there are fewer Dollars than Euros, that makes each Dollar worth more per Euro. If more Dollars were added back in, or Euros were taken out (or both), the Dollar side of the scale would drop and the line made by the market would fall.

The change in this six hour period is very small. At 13:00 our single US Dollar would buy us three thousandths of a Euro more than at 7:00. That doesn't sounds like a lot, and it isn't. But if, say, you were buying an apartment in Manhattan, and needed to exchange some Euros to pay for it, the tiny change shown by this chart would have a noticeable effect. We'll imagine the apartment cost a million US Dollars. At 7:00, a single US Dollar cost 0.764 Euros (I'm rounding down slightly for simplicity here). So a million US Dollars would cost 764,000 Euros. At the end of the chart, six hours later, a single US Dollar cost 0.767 Euros. So our million Dollars would now cost 767,000 Euros. The apartment effectively got three thousand Euros more expensive in six hours! Later we'll see how we can access big numbers like this, using small amounts of cash, to make big profits (or big losses if we're not careful).

What The Chart Is Really Telling Us

Before we continue looking at charts, let's take a minute to think about what this chart, and every other price chart, is telling us. Sure, it's showing the price of Euros in Dollars, but what does that mean? Remember, price is simply the value of something compared to money as perceived by the market. The price of a Euro in Dollars at any given moment, is the value in Dollars that everyone participating in the market thinks is a fair value for a Euro. If nobody thinks the current price is fair, no Euros will be sold, and the price will fall. If lots of people think it is fair, many Euros will be sold and those selling Euros will quickly see that they can command a higher price, so the price will rise.

So when we look at a chart like this, what we are actually looking at is a graph of market perception. Or put another way, we are looking at crowd psychology plotted as a line. Although traders deal with numbers all day, we're not really mathematicians. In fact we are more like psychologists or anthropologists. We're studying the behaviour of a large group, trying to predict its future actions from its past actions.

As we go through the rest of this book, try and keep that in mind. Every time you see a chart, don't think of it as just showing *prices*. Remind yourself that behind those prices are real people making real decisions about value. This will become more important when we start to look at the kinds of patterns that occur on these charts, because patterns are nothing more than markers of common crowd behaviour.

Why We Won't Use Line Charts

The chart we just looked at isn't showing us every possible price exchange rate between the US Dollar and the Euro in the six hour timeframe it occupies. A line chart like that is, necessarily, made up from a sample of data points, like this:

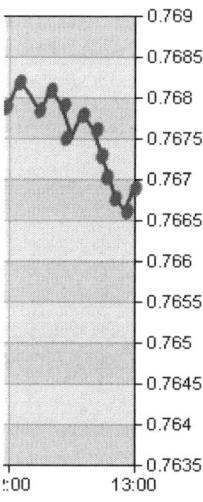

The price is sampled every few minutes, plotted on the chart, and the line connects the dots. The more times the price can be sampled and added to the chart, the more accurate it becomes. But there's a limit to how many points we can physically fit into a line chart like this before it becomes unreadable. That means we have to leave some price data out, and that presents a problem. How do we know we're not leaving out very important information? For example, if we decided to plot the price every 5 minutes and join those prices to make a line chart, what would happen if between 7:05 and 7:10 the price shot up to 0.769 for 2 minutes, then fell back down again? That could have happened on this chart, but we'll never know because that data didn't make it in. This lack of accuracy means we can't use line charts to make trading decisions from. If we did, we could be making decisions based on only a tiny proportion of the price information that is available to us.

Bar Charts

We can fit much more information onto the same size chart by using a *bar* chart. These are the staple of technical analysis, and are used the world over by traders of not just currencies, but also stocks, futures, bonds, and commodities. Here's what that previous line chart looks like when drawn as a bar chart:

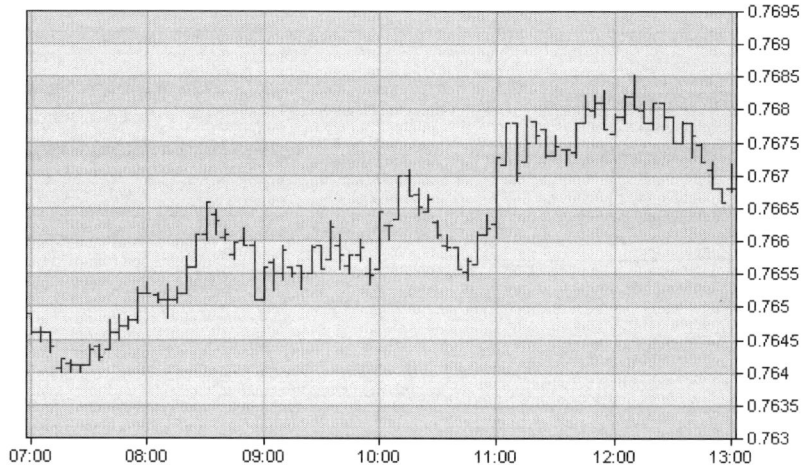

If you've never seen a chart like this before, don't panic! It looks like there's a lot going on but really it's very simple indeed. Instead of being made up of individual data points showing snapshots in time, this chart shows the full range of prices that the currency has reached. Every vertical bar on the chart is like a miniature line chart, squashed up into a single vertical line. Let's delve into a single bar to see how it's constructed, because each bar tells us quite a lot.

Consider the following sequence of USD/EUR prices:

0.7660 0.7650 0.7645 0.7655 0.7660
0.7665 0.7680 0.7675 0.7670 0.7665

Here's what that sequence looks like as a line chart:

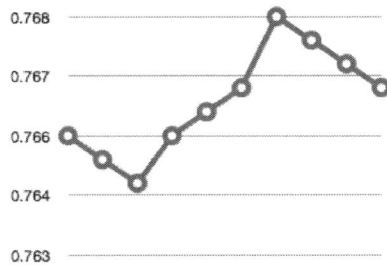

Each of the prices has been plotted and the line joins them together. If we wanted to plot every price that occurs throughout the day onto a single chart, our forex chart would quickly become gigantic, too big to be able to spot any patterns. The beauty of the bar chart is that we can compress a whole sequence of price points into a single bar. Here's how the sequence looks as a bar:

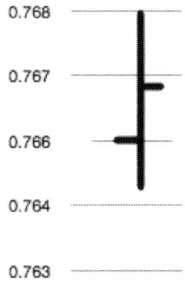

The bar, like a line chart, is read from left to right. The leftmost extremity tells us the price at the start of the bar, in this case 0.7660. The rightmost extremity tells us the price at the end of the bar, which was 0.7665. All the action in between has literally be squashed up into one vertical line. That means the line shows us the range that the price travelled in, the highest point it reached being 0.768 and the lowest point being 0.7645.

These price changes could have occurred over any length of time. They might have happened during 10 seconds, 10 minutes, 10 hours, or even 10 years. It doesn't matter how long a time period is represented, the bar will never take up more horizontal space. That means we can represent the full range of prices on a chart without the chart growing to gargantuan proportions horizontally.

Let's look at the last hour of our example chart as both a line chart and a bar chart, side by side. By the way, the bars in the example chart each represent a 5 minute period.

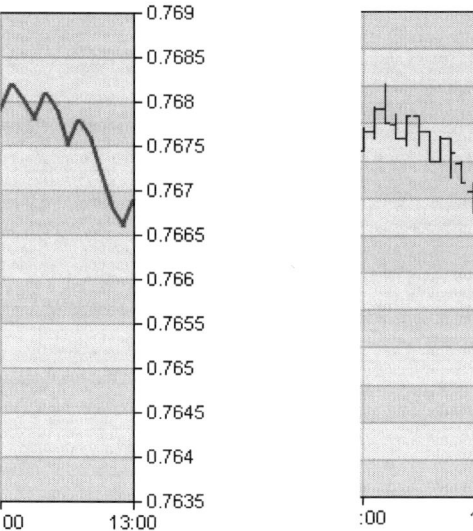

Now we can see the problem with the line chart more clearly. The highest price that the line chart arrived at was a shade over 0.768. Look at the third bar on the bar chart and we can see that actually the price got up to just a shade over 0.7685. That's not all; the final bar on the bar chart shows that the price was up over 0.767 before the end of the chart. But the line chart gives the impression that after the price fell below 0.767 it never got above it again. The bar chart packs in much more information in the same horizontal space.

Limitations of Bars

A bar then, covers all the prices that occurred during a fixed period of time. It shows us the price at the start and end of the period (we call these the *open* price and the *close* price), as well as the highest and lowest prices reached during the period (which we call simply the *high* and the *low*.)

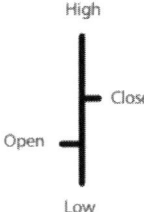

Although this bar shows us all the prices covered in a five minute period, we can only be sure about the order of two of them—the open and the close. We know that the price at the close (the end of the five minutes) was higher than the price at the open. We also know that at some point during those five minutes, it was higher still, and that at some other point, it was lower than at the open. What the bar doesn't tell us, is in what order these price changes happened. In other words, the bar above could have been formed from the sequence of numbers we looked at earlier, like this:

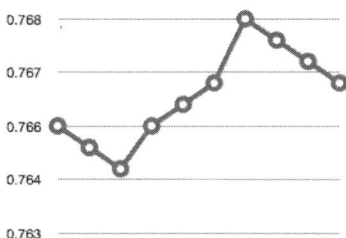

Or it could have formed quite differently, in fact, any of these sequences could have made that bar:

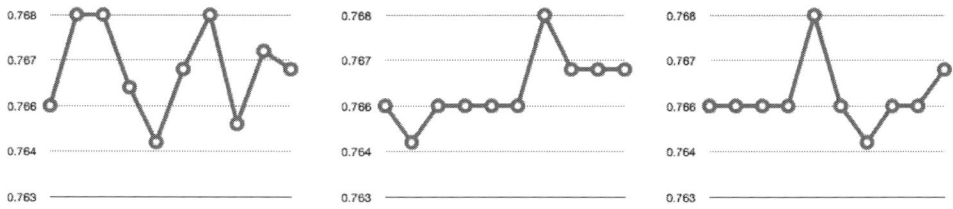

It's important not to make too many assumptions about what a bar is showing us. Bars in isolation give us useful information, but when we start looking at sequences of bars we can learn a lot more.

Bars In Context

As soon as we put bars together, we can begin to see patterns emerging, and we can start to try and make an educated guess about where the price of our chosen currency is headed. Not many conclusions could be drawn from our previous solitary bar. We know that over the five minute time period it summarises, the price ended up slightly higher than at the beginning, but on its own that information isn't very useful. What about if our bar was the third in this sequence of three bars?

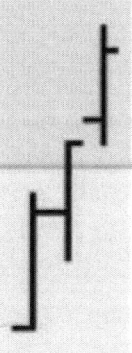

The preceding two bars both closed higher than they opened, as did our bar. There's a *trend* here—the price of the currency we're looking at in this chart is rising. If this was all the information we had to go on, it would be reasonable to guess that in the next bar the price is going to rise even higher. Of course it would be just that, a guess! It's entirely possible that on the next bar the price drops, or even stays just the same. But the fact the price has been rising up until this point, gives us just a hint that it may continue to do so.

As traders, we need to gather hints like this in order to make an informed opinion as to where the price is headed next. The more hints that point to the same thing, the greater the probability of that thing being right. We'll never be right in our opinion all the time, but remember we don't need to be. Being right just slightly more often than not, is enough to make a profit.

Candlesticks

Candlestick charts are an alternative way of presenting the same information shown in bar charts. Some people find them easier to read, others prefer the simplicity of bar charts.

A candlestick has three components: the thick *body* of the candle shows the open and close prices for the period covered. The thin *wick* protruding from the top extends to the highest price reached, and the thin *tail* sticking out the bottom extends to the lowest price. Here's what our example bar looks like as a candlestick.

As we can see, the four data points are just displayed slightly differently. But wait! There's a problem. How do we know if the *open* was higher than the *close*? With the bar, the open is always on the left and the close is always on the right, we always know which was which regardless of which was higher or lower. With the candle, the top and bottom of the body represent the open and close, there is no left and right. So how do we know which is which? Simple—if the body of the candle is empty, as with the candle above, then the open is at the bottom and the close is at the top. If the candle body is filled in, then the open was at the top and the close at the bottom. In other words a filled in candle shows us a time period where the price *fell*, and an empty candle shows us a period where the price *rose*. This simple visual cue is why many traders prefer candlesticks, they show the direction at a glance. Here's a candlestick where the price fell:

An alternative way of showing direction in candles is to fill the body with green if the price rose, and red if the price fell. In fact, most charting programs will let you set whatever colours you like. Here are some chart segments showing the same data as a bar chart, a black and white candlestick chart, and a red and green candlestick chart:

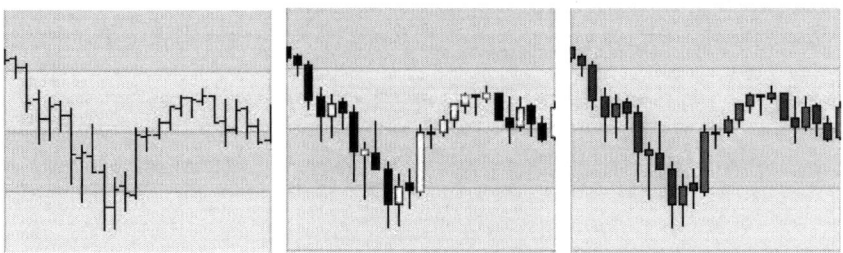

All three segments show exactly the same data. Candlestick charts *can* be slightly misleading in that the wider body of the candle draws the attention of the eye away from the wick. That means that when we glance at a candlestick chart, it's very easy to give more weight to the range shown by the body (i.e. the range between just the open and close prices), and discount the range of the wick. The solidity of the candle's body makes it appear more important than the thin wick above and below. But the range shown by the wick is actually more important, because that's the full range the price covered during the period of the candlestick. It's an easy trap to fall into, and for that reason I would suggest trying bar charts, simply because they to not exhibit this unusual bias. I will use examples of both throughout this book so you become familiar with each style.

Support & Resistance

Now that we know what a chart looks like, and how the bars or candles that go onto it are made, we can start to look for patterns in those bars. We will start by looking at support and resistance, which form the basis of many (but not all) patterns. Here's a chart segment, each bar is five minutes. I've left the scale off the chart because it's not important.

In the chart we can see that to begin with, the price is rising. Eventually it stops rising, and falls back down a bit. Then it goes back up, gets to pretty much where it managed before, then falls down again. It's almost like it has hit some kind of ceiling. We call this imagined ceiling *resistance*. We can draw it on the chart like this:

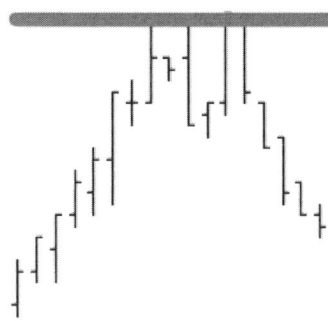

So what's going on here? Clearly there's no actual ceiling stopping the price from going any higher, so why is it behaving as if there were? To begin to understand, we need to remember that the chart is showing us price and that price is a perception of value as viewed by the majority within the market. So we're looking at a graph showing us the thoughts of a crowd of people. For the first seven bars, the perception of value is gradually rising. People are buying the currency we are charting (although it could equally be that this was a chart of the price of gold, or bread, or prawn salad sauce, it doesn't matter). On the eighth bar something changes, the price stops going up. The price has risen to a tipping point. The majority view has changed. The crowd has spoken, and they have said "enough!" They've stopped buying, which means the price can't get any higher. Either they don't think whatever they are buying is worth any more, or they don't believe it will be worth more in the future (future value perception), or both.

With not enough buyers around to enable them to raise the price, those wanting to sell have to drop it if they want to keep selling, and that's what happens on bar nine. On bar ten, the sellers try raising their prices again, but once again the buyers say "no!" The crowd's view of what is a fair price has not changed in that last five or ten minutes, and so they simply stop buying. The sellers are once again forced to lower their prices to keep selling, which we see happen on bars ten and eleven. On bars twelve and thirteen we see that the sellers make one final effort at pushing their price up. But the crowd view holds firm, and the buyers simply stop buying. Once again the sellers reduce their prices, and this time the price keeps on falling. By now the crowd may well have seen that they have the power to force the price back down. Those selling have tried, and failed, three times to raise their prices beyond this invisible ceiling. The crowd aren't dumb, they know that sooner or later the sellers will have to give up unless something happens in the meantime. Of course, something *could* happen quite easily, some small piece of news, some change in policy, some announcement. All the fundamental factors we looked at in the previous chapter are still at play. The crowd is watching those just like they are watching the price. For now though, the consensus view is that the price is too high, and that view is forcing it down. Here's how the chart continues:

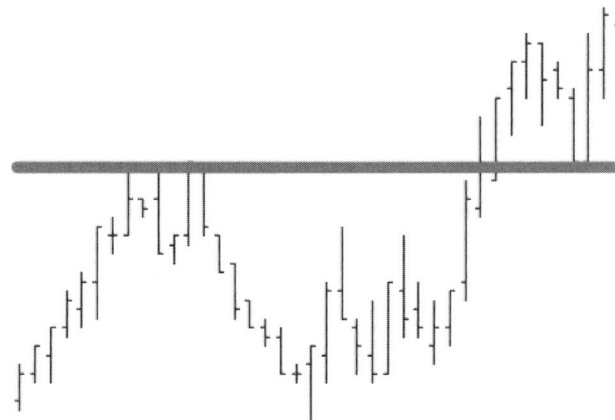

We can see that the price fell away, then there was a bit of backwards and forwards in opinion as it went up and down. About two thirds of the way along we see that the price rose quite sharply. It once again reached the invisible ceiling, the *resistance*, and for a short while the sellers were once again forced to drop their price. In the end though, the view of the crowd shifted, and enough became buyers to allow the price to continue to rise, breaking through the ceiling. Who knows what changed their minds? It could be that there was some news, or it could simply be that more people believed the price would rise and so now was a good time to buy. What is important is what happened next.

The price broke through the invisible ceiling and carried on going up for a few bars. Then it dropped suddenly, and quickly returned to that invisible ceiling. But it didn't go any lower. Why not? One reason is that anyone in the crowd who wanted to buy at that price but missed out the first time round, now has a second chance. If they take that opportunity to buy, it means more buyers in the market, which adds weight to the view that the price will rise. Another reason is that a lot of people decided to buy at that point (which is what enabled it to break through the ceiling). If they sell at that point or lower, they're going to be taking a loss on their investment. That means the crowd now includes a large number of potential sellers who have no desire to sell at that price. Fewer sellers means a rarer commodity, which means prices can rise.

Those are sound reasons the price may *bounce* at the previous resistance level. But there's another equally important reason, the self fulfilling prophecy I mentioned before. A large proportion of people making up the market, the crowd, will be looking at this chart. And they will see on it the same things that we can see. They will see the resistance, and they will see how the price broke through the resistance. And knowing that resistance often turns into *support*, they will interpret that as being a safe place to buy.

In part then, support and resistance occur because people are expecting it to occur, and believe certain things are more likely when it does. It sounds a little crazy, but actually this happens all the time in all areas of life. Apple launches a new iPhone and thousands of people think *"there will be huge long lines at the Apple store, and they will sell out on launch day, I'd better get in line!"* They duly get in line, thus creating the very lines they were predicting. Another example, the weather forecast says there's a snowstorm coming, roads might get blocked, deliveries to stores might be delayed. No need to panic, they say, the shops aren't going to run out of food. Half the population thinks *"They're gonna run out of food, time to panic buy!"*, and heads for the stores, causing them to run out of food.

How Does This Help Us?

Ultimately it doesn't matter if all this is crazy behaviour or not. What *is* important is that it happens, and the consequences of this crowd mentality are what cause the patterns we see on the chart. This is why it is so important to view the chart as the actions of the crowd, not simply as some nebulous concept of price. It shows us real actions that real people are taking. Think like the crowd, and we can begin to predict its next move, just like the example above of the resistance area turning into support.

How might that be useful to us? If we see something like that previous chart snippet, a resistance area that gets broken and then the price bouncing off it turning to support, that tells us there's a pretty good probability the price is going to go up again. It looks like the crowd don't want it dropping below that previous resistance area (now a support area), so it's more likely to either stay much the same, or go upwards. Knowing that to be the case gives us a good opportunity to *buy*, with a view to selling at a higher price for a profit. And because plenty of other traders will see the same thing, lots of them will take the opportunity to buy as well, helping push the price up! Yes, *you and I* are part of the crowd too. We're all looking at the same thing, and when enough of us interpret it in the same way, it's going to have predictable consequences. We truly are the masters of our own destiny when we trade.

We can call a pattern like this a *buy signal*. It is a signpost pointing the way to a place where we might want to buy. Of course, buying with a view to sell on at a profit is only half the story, we need to decide when the right time to sell is. As you might have guessed, we could use a *sell signal* to do that. The same pattern in reverse would make a good sell signal, and there are plenty more we're going to discover as we go along.

MISSION: From today, try spotting support and resistance on currency price charts (check the Resources page for an up to date list of places you can get free charts). If you can, print some out and physically draw on the support and resistance lines, it will help you identify them more easily. Or you can use the tools provided on the charting websites to draw lines on screen. Look at a new chart every day. With practice it will become second nature to spot these support and resistance areas. As this is a skill at the heart of trading, it's worth working to acquire that skill from today.

Trends

When price bars (or candlesticks) over a period of time make continually higher highs and higher lows, or they make continually lower highs and lower lows, we say that the price is *trending*. We can draw support or resistance lines on charts that are trending upwards or downwards, we call these angled lines *trend lines*. Here's an example of an upwardly trending price, with a support trend line drawn in underneath:

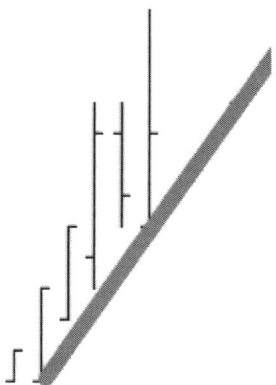

As we can see from this chart, the *low* prices of the bars are, on average, rising with each bar. The high prices are also, on average, rising. When this happens, we say that the price is *trending* upwards (an *up trend*). If we can connect several of these lows together with a straight line, as has been done in the example, we have a *trend line*. When the trend is upwards, this is effectively a form of support, and behaves just like the horizontal support line we just looked at. The line can be drawn in as soon as there are enough bars to suggest its existence, there are no hard and fast rules about how many bars must be connected to make the trend line. It needs to be at least two, but three or more is better. The trend line, as with a regular horizontal support line, can be predictive. It gives us a clue that the price may well continue upwards. By extending the trend line beyond the end of the chart (as above), we can see the lowest prices that future bars are likely to make. As you might have figured out, a prediction like this can give us an opportunity to trade. We're looking for clues about where the price is headed next, and the trend line here is suggesting that it is upwards. If we were to buy while the price was close to the trend line, we would have a better than 50% chance of it subsequently rising. Let's see how that chart continued:

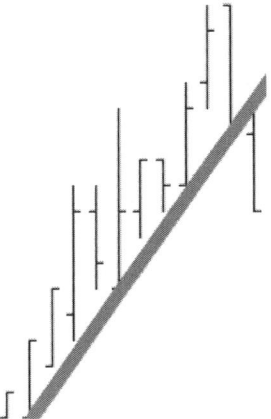

The price did indeed continue upwards, and *bounced* off the trend line a couple more times. Eventually it dropped through. Before starting its decent though, as we can see from the final bar, it rose and touched the line before falling back. So just like with the horizontal resistance line becoming *support*, so this upwards support trend line became resistance after it was breached.

The reasons this up trend line works are exactly the same as the reasons a regular support line is effective. As the price rises, a number of traders will be looking to buy with a view to selling higher. When it falls back, this presents an opportunity to buy at a relatively good price. Those purchases cause the price to rise again, and an up trend is born. As more people see the trend and start drawing or imagining trend lines on their charts, an element of self fulfilling prophecy comes into play and the line takes on a life of its own.

How Trends Are Useful

There are two ways a trend line like this could be useful to us as we look to start a new trade. The first I alluded to above. Newton's first law of motion tells us that *every body persists in its state of being at rest or of moving uniformly straight forward, except insofar as it is compelled to change its state by force impressed*. In other words, if something is still, it will stay still until something exerts some force on it to move it. When something is moving, it's going to keep moving until something comes along to change that. This law applies largely to prices as well. Once price is established in a trend, it will continue that trend until some external force changes things. That external force is buying or selling pressure. When it comes to our up trending price, we can assume it will continue rising until there is a sufficient change in the balance of buying and selling to stop the rise. Put another way, when the price is rising, it's easier for it to keep on rising than it is for it to stop, or to start dropping. The *probability* of a price continuing to rise once it is established in an up trend is greater than the probability of it dropping. Our mission as traders is to try and weigh up probabilities like this, to determine where the price might be headed next. This up trend tips the balance of probability. If we have a better than 50% chance that the price is going up, then clearly the odds favour *buying* now with a view to *selling* at a higher price. There is more chance of making money by buying in an up trend than there is by selling. So we can say that once the trend line is established, by connecting together the low of at least two bars (and preferably at least three), we have a *signal* to buy. If we were to make the assumption that the price is going to keep rising, it would be advantageous to execute our buy while the price was as close to the line as possible, as that would be the time the price was at its lowest, giving the greatest headroom for a rise. In the chart segment above, a good place to buy might be near the lowest points of the eighth or ninth bar.

If we followed a signal like this and executed an order to buy, and the price subsequently dropped below the trend line, we would know that the up trend had been broken. An external force (selling pressure) would have acted on the price sufficiently strongly to arrest its rise. It would no longer be the case that the probability of the price continuing to rise would be higher than 50%. Such a break of the line would be a *signal* to exit the trade we had entered, by selling back what we had bought.

So trend lines can help us decide when to buy, by pointing out up trends to us. They can also help us decide when to sell by showing us when an up trend has come to an end. These *sell* signals can be used to enter new trades just as they can be used to exit existing ones. We can sell now with a view to buying back at a lower price, profiting from the difference (short selling).

Trends Within Trends

Everything that applies to up trends applies equally to down trends. When we draw a trend line on a down trend, we link the highs of the bars or candlesticks instead of the lows, like this:

Although this is a candlestick chart rather than the bar charts used in the previous example, we see that the information provided is the same. In this example, like the up trend example before, the trend is quite tight, the price bars and candles stay close to the trend line. That doesn't always happen, sometimes the price moves much further away then comes back to the line.

In this chart we see a trend form over a much longer period of time. In fact, if we look closer at this particular chart, we can see that there are trends within trends. Long before we could ever draw that long down trend line, there is an earlier down trend we could draw in:

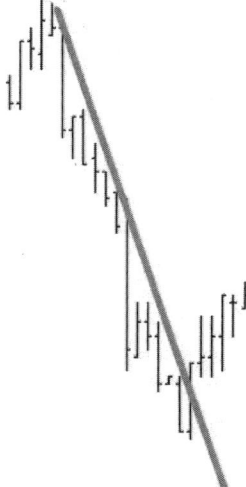

At this early stage of the chart we have no idea about that long term down trend, but we can see another steep down trend which we can draw on. Eventually that trend is broken, and the price looks to start going up.

Indeed as time goes on, an up trend establishes itself:

Eventually that trend gets broken, and the price looks to start heading down again. Now we can draw in the longer term down trend line that we saw in the first chart:

The chart is now telling us two important pieces of information:

1) The price was most recently in a short term up trend, and that trend appears to have been broken.

2) There could be a longer term down trend forming.

These are two signals which both tell us that probability is on the side of the price dropping. One signal is good, two is always better. Taken together, these can be seen as a stronger signal that the price is going to fall, at least in the short term. As we've already seen, that is exactly what happened:

In fact the price dropped quite quickly here. We can of course, draw in another trend line to highlight that drop. That new line gets broken a few times, and then the price goes back up, where it duly *bounces* off our longer term down trend line. We can even draw in a trend line for that last little run up:

This final up trend line gives us another double signal that the price is likely to fall when it gets broken, and does so at the point where the price is bouncing off the longer term down trend. Two signs that the price may fall, both occurring at exactly the same time. Naturally, plenty of other traders will see these signals, and will reach the same conclusion—the price looks set to fall. Probability is clearly stacked on the side of a price drop, and indeed that is what happens.

As this chart segment shows, there are trends within trends. The price might be in an up trend at a given moment, but zoom out and look at the bigger picture and you may well find that longer term it is in a down trend. Zoom out further still, and that down trend might just be a small part of an even longer term up trend! How far out should we look? The answer depends on the timescale we are trading in. If we truly are *day trading*, looking to exit our trade before the end of the day, then there is little point in looking at trends that are occurring over months or years, they will have little impact on what happens during a single day. But a trend lasting a few days could have an impact. The takeaway message here is that when looking at charts, we should always be trying to identify any trends, short and longer term. Try and see the bigger picture as well as the more immediate action. If we trade in the same direction as a trend, we have the *momentum*, and thus the odds, stacked a little more in our favour. We're swimming with the flow of the river as it were. In fact it is perfectly possible to be profitable just from taking trades based on trend lines like those above. But we can do better than that, we can put the odds even more in our favour by looking for more signals. We'll see how as we go on.

MISSION: From today onwards, in addition to looking for support and resistance areas on currency price charts, start looking for trend lines. Try and identify short term and longer term trends. Spotting these is another core skill in trading, and one well worth working on for a few minutes every day.

The Big Picture

Prices don't spend all their time trending upwards or downwards, a lot of the time they are just drifting. Zoom out though, and you'll find that even drifting prices are part of a bigger overall trend. When we look at any price chart, our first thought should be to try and identify the big picture—the overall direction of the price—up, down, or sideways. We want to get an overview of the general long term direction, as well as any short term trends that are happening right now. We want to spot any areas of support or resistance, and see if there are any immediately obvious patterns like triangles or double tops or bottoms (more on those in a moment), that might give a clue as to any imminent change in direction. The more obvious any trend, support or resistance area, or pattern, the more traders are going to see it. The more traders who see something, the more who are likely to act on it, and that means the more predictable the chart is. We're looking at the actions of real people, trying to figure out what they are going to do next. Soon we'll look at some other signals we can use to predict price movements with a greater granularity. But we should never lose sight of the big picture.

Patterns

Now we know how to find support, resistance, and trends on price charts, we can start to look for patterns. Because prices move as a result of the actions of people (buying and selling) and people are prone to habit and repetition, we tend to see certain patterns repeat themselves on charts. If we see a pattern that is known to recur, then we have a good signal for what is going to happen next. Just as we can predict that if the government tells people not to start panic buying groceries, people will start panic buying, so we can predict that if we see a common pattern on a chart, people will react to it the same way they always do.

We're going to look at three very common patterns here. Like everything else we've examined so far, these patterns are largely about seeing the big picture. They give us further indications as to where price is headed next. Whilst it is perfectly possible to use these patterns in isolation as buy and sell signals, we will go further and add an extra layer of refinement over the top later on.

Triangles

Triangles occur when the price becomes constrained by a combination of two trend lines (one up and one down), or a trend line and either a support or a resistance line. Here's an example:

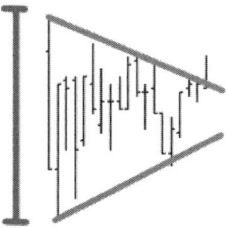

Here the price appears to be in a down trend (as shown by the down trend line) and an up trend, at the same time. This is a classic sign of indecision in the market. There is no general consensus as to whether price is rising or falling. As time progresses, price becomes more and more constrained, there is more and more indecision. Two things could occur:

1) This indecision continues, and the price continues to oscillate in a small range.
2) A consensus view becomes predominant and the price begins to rise or to fall.

In either case, the price will eventually break through one or both of the trend lines that form the triangle. If the price breaks out before it gets totally squeezed, then this is a strong sign that consensus has been reached and the price is going to continue in the direction in which it broke through, as is the case in the chart segment above. If on the other hand, the price breaks through the lines simply by virtue of the fact it is going sideways and there's no room left between the trend lines, then that suggests no consensus has yet been reached.

In the case of a consensus view and a break of the triangle (called a *breakout*), the triangle pattern itself provides a clue as to just how far the price is going to continue in its new direction. The price difference between the low and high at the start of the triangle is roughly the distance the price is likely to travel. This isn't a hard and fast rule, after all, nobody knows for sure what is going to happen. But it does occur frequently enough that we can say there is a higher probability of the price continuing that distance than it not doing so. Based on that probability, here is where we think the price has a good chance of going in our example:

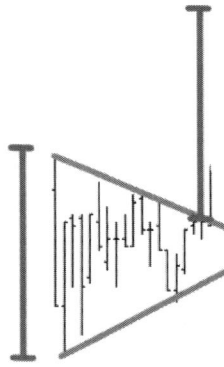

This is a possible buy signal. We know there is a good chance that the price is going to increase by the amount shown by the vertical line. Let's see what happened next:

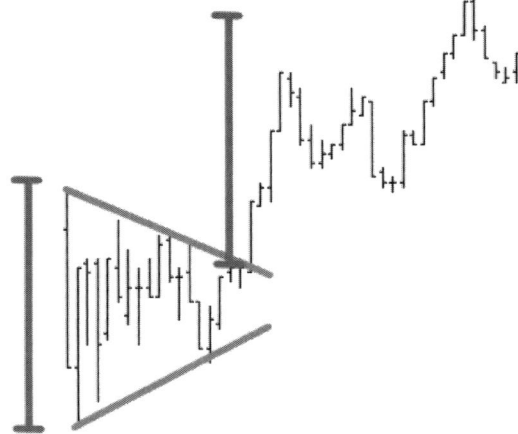

The price continued upwards, and eventually reached the level predicted by the triangle pattern. It didn't go there straight away, it fell short and even started to fall back, but it got there in the end. If we had bought at the moment the price broke out of the pattern, we could have sold at the *target* price suggested by the triangle, for a healthy profit.

Let's look at another example:

This time the triangle is made up of a regular horizontal resistance line at the top, and an up trend line at the bottom. Once again the price breaks through before it simply reaches the end of the pattern, breaking the lines by virtue of continuing sideways. That gives us the clue that this breakout shows a consensus has been reached. More traders think the price is going down than think it's going up.

Notice that this triangle occurred as the price was in an up trend. Because it broke out to the bottom, we are now expecting the price to descend. It looks like the pattern is showing us a change of trend. If we had previously bought and were *long*, then the breakout of this triangle would be a very good time to sell and exit our trade before the price falls further. If we weren't already in a trade, it would be a good opportunity to sell *short* with a view to buying later at a lower price, realising a profit.

Consolidation

Triangle patterns always include at least one trend line, and may include a horizontal support or resistance line. Prices can also become constrained by two horizontal lines, one each of support and resistance. This is a *consolidation* pattern, also called a *rectangle*. Here's an example:

In this chart segment, the price is trending upwards. It stops that up trend, drops a little, before going up again. It doesn't get very far before it falls back. However, it doesn't get any lower than it did during its previous fall. At that point we can draw in a horizontal *support* line. The price then rises, and gets as far as its previous *high* point, before falling away. That's the point at which we can draw in a horizontal resistance line, between the last two highs. It's now pretty clear that the price is constrained between these two lines, something that becomes even more apparent when it bounces off the support line for a third time. After that it quite suddenly pushes upwards, breaking out of the pattern and continuing its rise.

Consolidation patterns often occur after frantic periods of buying or selling. Participants in the market become wary of the recent price movement. Those who have been buying in an up trend for example, may wish to lock in some of their profit by selling their position. Enough selling will cause the price to drop. But the rise might not yet be over, and if enough people think it's going higher, they will push it back up. This can continue as buyers and sellers offload their positions and enter new positions, pushing the price up and down. All the mechanics of support and resistance are at work, just in close proximity. The price can either continue to drift sideways, or it will break out of the pattern. As with the triangle, the manner in which it effects its breakout gives us a clue as to where it is going next. If the price simply drifts outside the bounding lines, it isn't really telling us anything, there is no clear consensus view on its direction. If on the other hand, the price pushes through one of the lines with force and determination—as is the case in the example above, where it moves strongly upwards in the space of a single bar—that is a sign that there is a strong consensus view on direction, and a good chance the price will continue to move in that direction. Indeed we see that is what happened above.

Rectangle consolidation patterns provide the same signals and opportunities to us as their triangle cousins. By showing us the likely direction of the price, at least in the short term, we can make a decision as to whether we might want to buy or sell, whether we want to enter a new trade, or exit an existing one.

If we were using a pattern like this to signal the entry of a new trade, we should be mindful of the big picture. If the price is showing an overall up trend, then a breakout upwards (as above) would be a stronger signal to enter a new trade than a breakout downwards. Not only would we have the breakout itself suggesting rising prices, but we would be in a trend upwards which would help carry those prices higher. We'd be swimming with the current, not against it. We would have probability in our favour. That's not to say we shouldn't use a break to the downside as an entry signal, it simply means that a confluence of signals (the existing up trend and the breakout upwards) are a more powerful signal of rising prices than just one signal taken in isolation. This is why we should always keep an eye on the big picture, why we should always know the overall trend.

Double Tops

We've seen already how prices can trend, making a series of higher highs and higher lows (an up trend) or series of lower highs and lower lows (a down trend). A high occurs when a bar reaches a price higher than the bars either side of it. A low occurs when a bar reaches a price lower than the bars either side of it. Here's a chart segment showing both an up trend and a down trend:

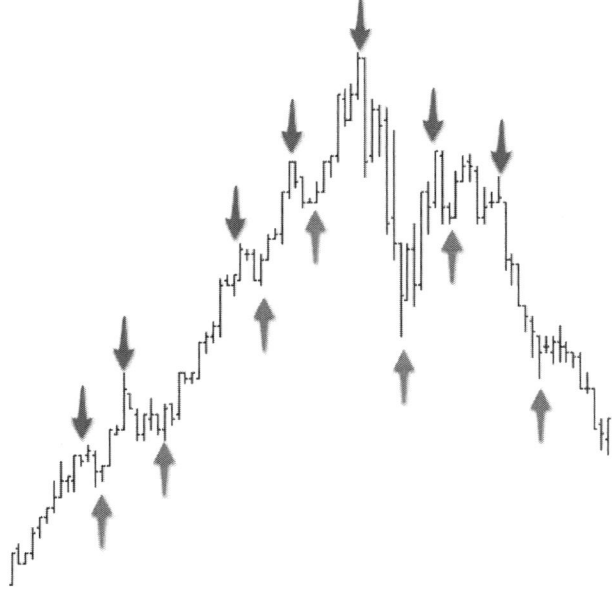

The lows on this chart are indicated by the up arrows below the bars, and the highs are shown by the down arrows above the bars. The price starts off in an up trend, it is making a series of higher highs and higher lows. After peaking at the fifth high, it starts a down trend, making a series of lower highs and lower lows. The point at which the price transitions from the up trend to the down trend is a pattern called a *double top*. This is simply the price making a lower high after it has previously been making consistently higher highs. Here's the double top again, with the label 1 showing the final high in the sequence of higher highs, and the label 2 showing the next high, which is lower than the previous one:

A double top doesn't necessarily mean that a new down trend has started, it just means that the pure and technical definition of an up trend is at an end. For an up trend to continue it must make higher highs, and at point 2 on the chart above, it failed to do that. At this point the price can either move sideways, or start going back up (making new highs and thus beginning a new up trend), or it may fall, making new lows and thus starting a down trend. Given that two out of the three possible scenarios involve the price *not* going up any more, we can say there is a lower probability of the price rising than not rising. Therefore if we were in a *long* trade (i.e. we bought with a view to selling higher), a double top pattern would be a good signal to sell and exit our trade.

Double Bottoms

Everything that applies to double tops does of course, apply equally in reverse. In a down trend (a series of lower highs and lower lows), the failure to make a new lower low will create a *double bottom*:

Point 1 above shows the lowest low. The low at point 2 is higher than that at point 1, which means by definition the down trend has ended. The price may start a new down trend, continue to rise, or just drift sideways. There is a lower probability that price will go back down than not go back down, so a double bottom pattern can be seen as a signal to exit a short trade. Whether or not we are in a trade when this pattern occurs, we should see it as an alert that the big picture could be changing. The price could be shifting into a new direction.

MISSION: In addition to looking for support, resistance, and trends on currency charts each day, start looking for triangle patterns, as well as double tops and double bottoms. Getting familiar with these patterns will help you to be able to spot them at a glance in the future.

Timescales

So far most of the chart segments we've been looking at have not included a scale, either horizontal or vertical. In fact, for everything we have covered so far, the horizontal scale—the time scale—is irrelevant. It doesn't matter whether the bars or candlesticks in those charts represent 1 minute each, 10 minutes, an hour, a day, or even a month each. The patterns and formations work exactly the same in any time frame. Of course, the smaller the amount of time represented by each bar, the more detail we see. Consider this chart:

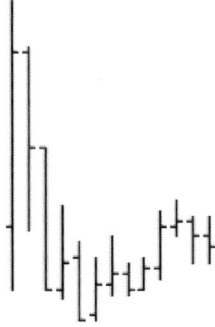

This is a 30 minute chart, i.e. each bar represents 30 minutes, so the chart covers six and a half hours. Whilst we can see the full range covered by the price during that time, and we can even draw in a small up trend line from the middle to the end, there is a limited amount of data. The very first bar for example, covered a huge range, almost as much as the rest of the chart. What happened during that time? To find out, we can switch to a more granular chart, like this:

This chart covers exactly the same time period as the first, but now each bar represents 5 minutes instead of 30. Using this more detailed chart, we can look inside the bars of the 30 minute chart. The first 30 minute bar, for example, is now shown as six 5 minute bars. We can see that half of the price rise during that 30 minute period, actually occurred within the first five minutes. Looking further along the chart, we can see that the low point in the middle of the 30 minute chart was hit five times by five consecutive 5 minute bars. From the 30 minute chart, we had no idea if the price hit that low once, or a hundred times. Seeing the detail in the 5 minute chart shows us there were at least five bounces, which indicates to us that there was pretty strong support at that level. Finally the second half of the 5 minute chart shows the new up trend in greater detail. But lets get back to the start of the chart, as that's where most of the action appears to be. We can go even deeper, and look at a 1 minute chart of the same period:

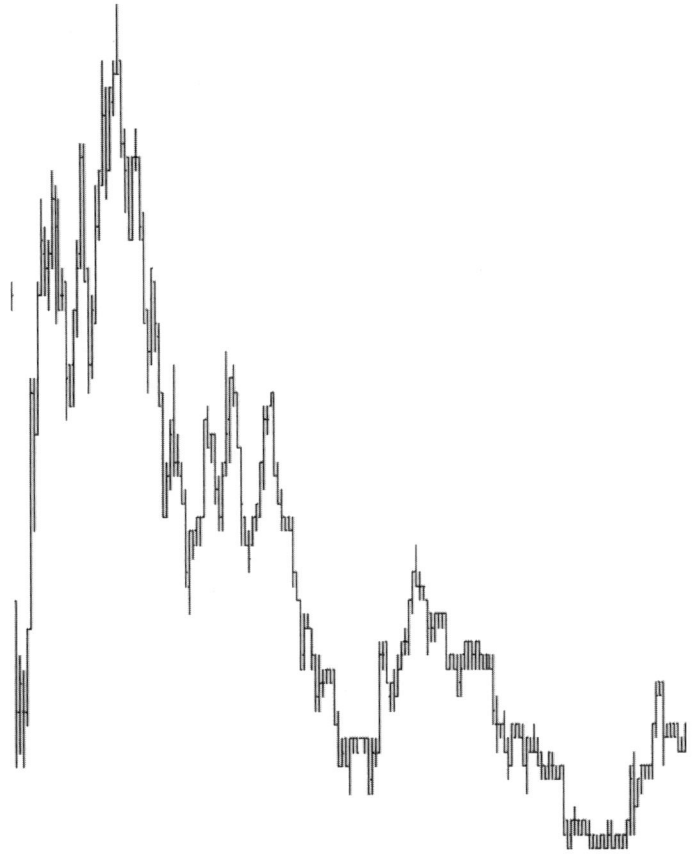

Now each bar represents 1 minute. Only the first half of the chart is shown here, as it's getting pretty big! Having zoomed in to this level, we can see that in fact the price didn't rise immediately, it took a few minutes to get going, rose quickly for 2 minutes, then faltered a little. Near the end of this chart, we can see that support line being formed in even more detail.

Choosing Timescales

This ability to zoom in, fractal-like, and examine the micro detail in charts is all well and good, and can be very useful for confirming support and resistance areas, as in the above example. But for most of our trading, we should choose one timescale and stick to it. Jumping around between scales can lead to confusion, it can cause us to over analyse every situation. How do we decide which timescale to use? Simple, we choose one that fits the time frame we are trading in. We are looking for patterns that will give us clues as to the future direction of the price, and we need a certain number of bars for a pattern to form. A triangle pattern, for example, might take ten or fifteen bars to form, and double that number once it breaks out, to reach its price target. If we are looking at 5 minute bars, those ten to fifteen bars are going to take an hour or two to form, and up to four hours for the price to reach its target. If we are looking at ten minute bars, obviously that's going to take twice as long for our pattern to form. And if we use daily bars, where each bar represents one full day, then it could take two weeks for a triangle just to form! Clearly if we are day trading, then there is little point in using daily charts. That's not to say daily charts are of no use. They work exactly the same as 5 minute charts, but because they are encompassing a much larger timescale, the vertical scale—the price scale—is also much larger. In other words a pattern made on a daily chart will have a much higher price target than the same pattern on a 5 minute chart. A trade made from a daily chart will take days or weeks from start to end, but the profit potential is proportionally larger than the same type of trade made from a 5 minute chart.

As this book is focussed on day trading, I am recommending the use of either 5 minute or 10 minute *intraday* charts (any chart whose timescale is less than one day is called an intraday chart). These provide ample granularity and detail, without losing sight of the bigger picture. Patterns that we see on charts in these scales are perfectly tradable within our time frame. There is another reason for choosing these scales, and that is that they are very commonly used. Remember, we are watching the actions of real market participants, we're trying to figure out what they are thinking and what they will do next. We want to see the same thing those other participants are seeing. We are trying to guess the actions of the crowd, and to best do that, we need to be looking at the same thing as the crowd. If we are looking at a 7 minute chart (perfectly possible) but most of the rest of the market is watching a 5 minute chart, we are not going to see the same thing. A pattern that is beautifully clear and obvious on the 5 minute chart, may well pass us by on our unusual 7 minute chart.

MISSION: As you look at currency charts daily, looking for support, resistance, trends, and patterns, try changing the time scale of those charts. Look for patterns in different time scales, and see how long they take to complete, and the sort of price distance they cover relative to other time scales.

Price Scale

Time occupies the horizontal scale of our price charts, and price inhabits the vertical scale. There are two distinct scales we can use to indicate price, *linear* and *logarithmic*. The linear price scale is the basic scale you would expect. Price increments are shown in equal graduations. If the distance between, for example, 1.12 and 1.13 (i.e. a price difference of 0.01) is one centimetre on the chart, then the distance between 2.23 and 2.24 will also be one centimetre, because the price difference is still 0.01.

With the *logarithmic* scale on the other hand, the physical distance between prices on the chart is not constant. Instead, the distance is representative of the percentage difference between two prices. So using our previous example, if the distance between 1.12 and 1.13 was one centimetre, that centimetre represents not a price difference of 0.01, but a *percentage* difference between those prices of 0.9%. When the chart reaches the lofty heights of 2.23, our price difference between 2.23 and 2.24 is still 0.01, but as a percentage of price that difference is 0.45%, which is half the percentage difference between the previous two prices. Therefore on the chart using the logarithmic scale, the distance between 2.23 and 2.24 would only be half a centimetre.

The difference is a subtle one, but it can be useful for getting a bigger picture view of large price movements by keeping the distance covered by bars and candlesticks proportional to the percentage change in prices. Here's a chart segment shown as a regular linear chart on the left, and a logarithmic scaled chart (often referred to as simply a log chart) on the right:

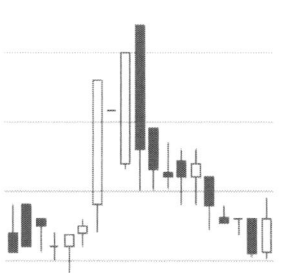 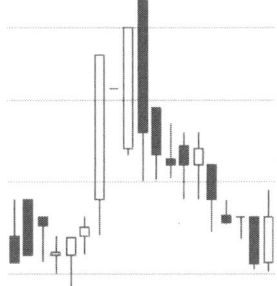

Not a huge difference, but the logarithmic chart better shows the range covered by the 12th, 13th, and 14th bars in proportion to the preceding bars, compared to the linear chart. I mention log charts simply for completeness, but I don't recommend using them for two reasons. One is the same reason I don't recommend using 7 minute charts or anything else out of the ordinary. The vast majority of market participants will be looking at linear charts, and we need to see what they see, so that we can try and read what they will do next. Any deviation from that will reduce our chances of getting inside the collective mindset of the market. The second, more practical reason, is that in the world of forex where we are dealing in relatively tiny price changes (down in the decimal places), the difference between log and linear charts is minimal (particularly on intraday charts) as the above example demonstrates. There's simply not enough of a benefit to using log charts to make it worth locating the setting in the charting software.

Indicators

Price bars and candlesticks show us a summary of price changes over time, and we can use different time scales to summarise those changes to a greater or lesser degree. We can go further though, by summarising price bars and candlesticks themselves. We do this by performing calculations on the values of bars and overlaying the results of those calculations on the price chart. We call these overlaid calculations *indicators*. There are a whole raft of indicators, and it is beyond the scope of this book to explain each and every one. What is more important is to understand the principles behind them, and their uses.

Before we continue, I must say that I am not a huge fan of indicators per se. They can be useful in certain circumstances, and we will be using them when we get into detailed trading strategies. A lot of traders become too reliant on them though, to the point where they forget their purpose, and even their meaning.

Indicators are really just tools to help us to spot certain things on the chart. Like any tool, their existence does not imply we must use them all the time, or even at all. A GPS unit is a tool which can help us get from A to B, but it doesn't replace the need to understand how to read the road ahead when driving. If we became overly reliant on our GPS to the point where we stopped looking out of the window, we would be shooting red lights, running into the back of slow moving vehicles, and would quickly become lost as soon as there was some detour caused by roadworks, or an error in the GPS map. Indicators are the same. They can provide assistance in navigating a price chart, but it's important to keep looking at that chart, both to confirm what the indicator is suggesting, and also to see things it can't tell us.

There's another reason to be wary of indicators. Continuing the GPS analogy, if we had two or three GPS units in the car, and each one chose a slightly different route to get to our destination, life would quickly become very confusing. When we reached a junction and one GPS said to go left, and another said go right, we would be worse off than having no GPS at all! Using too many indicators can cause the very same problem. It is entirely possible to find certain indicators which will suggest the price may rise, whilst others will be suggesting a fall is imminent. Combining indicators *can* be a good thing. Like combining a GPS and a good old fashioned map which can be used to confirm the route chosen by the gadget, combining one indicator with another which is suitably complimentary can allow us to confirm trade signals. Understanding how indicators work then, is essential as it will help us choose which, if any, to combine for our chosen trading strategy.

Moving Averages

A moving average is one of the most simple indicators that can be calculated on price. As its name would suggest, a moving average (often abbreviated to MA) is an average price value that moves with price. Let's look at an example which will make this clear.

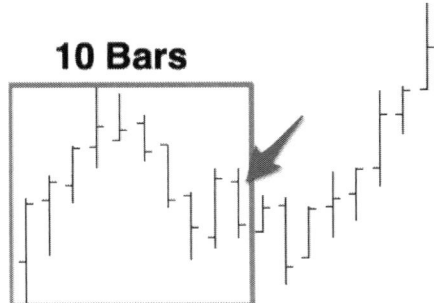

To calculate the first point in the moving average, we must calculate the average price over the last *n* bars. We are going to plot a 10 period moving average, which is to say, the average price for the previous 10 bars. We can calculate that price in a number of ways. We could add up the *last* price of the last ten bars and divide by ten. We could add up the *open* price of the last ten bars and divide that by ten. Or we could use the *high* or *low* prices of the bars. A better way though, is to use the average price of each bar. We get that by adding together the *high, low,* and *close* of a bar and dividing the result by three (it's not a true average, it is slightly weighted towards the close price, but it is a common calculation). We make that calculation for each bar, we add the results together for the last ten bars, then divide by ten. The result of all that is an average price over that ten bar period, which we can plot on the chart when the tenth bar closes. In the example above, we can estimate the average price of the first ten bars (bound by the box) will fall roughly where the arrow is pointing. As the next bar starts, we can re-do the calculation for the previous ten bars. Below we see the average of *those* ten bars is going to be a little higher, because we're no longer counting the first bar which was lower than all the others. The arrow shows roughly where the next point on the moving average will be.

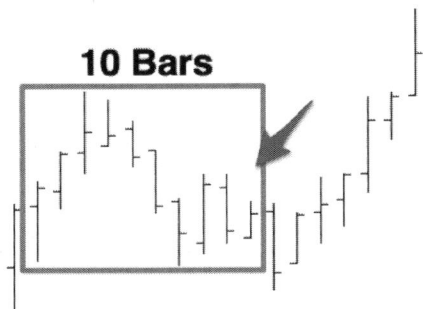

As the chart progresses, we continue the calculation, always using the previous ten bars and plotting the result at the close of the current bar. The plot points are joined together to form a continuous line. Here's what the chart looks like when the moving average is overlaid:

Because the moving average is based on previous price activity, there is a delay—or a lag—between that activity and its inclusion in the indicator. For that reason we call this a *lagging* indicator. It is summarising what has already happened. That can be useful to us for a number of reasons. Firstly, it gives us a very quick way to spot price trends. When looking at a chart with lots of bars going up, down, and sideways, it isn't always obvious if there is a trend, and if so, where. A moving average line smooths out all of that movement and gives us a *bigger picture* overview. Have a look at this chart segment, first naked and pure, and then with a 10 period moving average added:

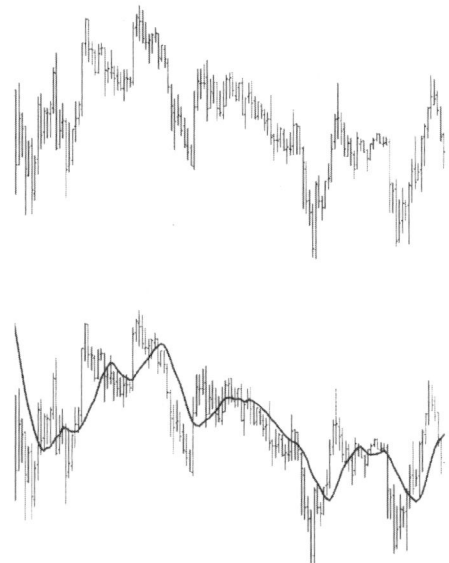

The moving average line makes it easy to see the overall rise and fall of the price. Not only that, at the end of the chart the moving average highlights a double bottom pattern. Of course we can still see the pattern on the naked price chart, but as it's not as pristine and clean an example as that we looked at earlier, it's not as easy to spot. The moving average shouts it out. It's not just the double bottom that the moving average calls out, we can also look for support, resistance, trend lines, and patterns. This example chart shows us a support line around the double bottom, and there's a down trend line too:

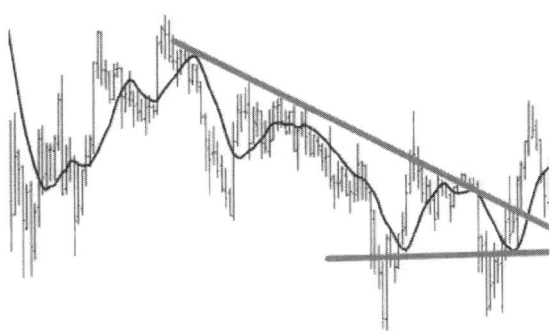

It is easier to see these lines and patterns on the moving average because it is a clean flowing line rather than a whole bunch of price bars. There's a downside of course; because the indicator lags the price, by the time the moving average breaks out of that nice triangle pattern above, the price has already moved on and risen. The breakout of the triangle as drawn on the moving average is suggesting a price rise, but that price rise has already begun. If we wanted to enter a trade to profit from it, it looks like we already missed a lot of the action! This is one of the reasons indicators should be used with such caution, they only tell you what already happened.

There is another reason indicators like moving averages can be useful, and that comes back to the herd mentality of the market. A lot of traders use them, and as we know, we need to see what other traders are seeing. We need to think like the herd, so we can predict its next move. Because so many traders look at moving averages, they have a certain self-fulfilling property. Moving averages can actually become support and resistance lines in themselves. We'll see examples of that happening later on.

So far we've just looked at a moving average calculated over ten price bars. Why ten? Why not 20, 30, or 36? Indeed we can use any number we like. The more price bars we use in the calculation, the more *laggy* the indicator becomes. The slower it is to react to sudden price changes. On the other hand, the better it summarises the action.

Here's our sample chart again with two different moving averages plotted.

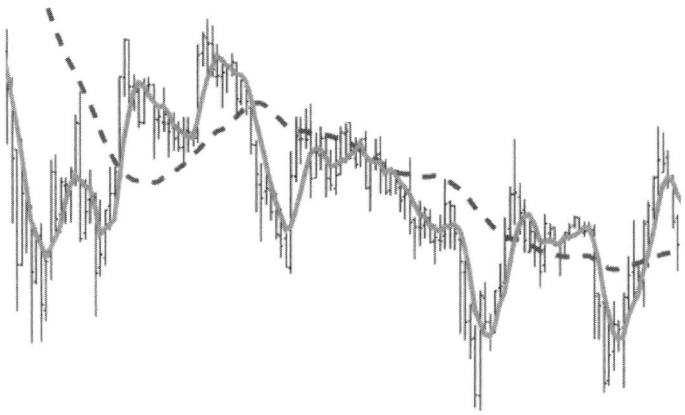

The dashed moving average is calculated using 30 bars, and the solid one uses just 5 bars. The longer average is much slower to react to price changes. It gives a very high level overview of the price direction. It would be hard to take trading decisions based on that moving average alone, it's just too slow.

The 5 period average on the other hand, follows the price very closely. It reacts quickly to price changes, showing us more detail about the trends within trends. On the other hand, it isn't giving us much benefit over just looking at the price itself.

Moving Average Trading Strategies

We can use moving averages to come up with all sorts of trading strategies—methods for deciding when to enter and exit trades. The simplest signal we could use based on a moving average is to buy when the price crosses above it, and sell when the price drops below it. The fewer the number of periods used in the MA, the more signals we'll get, but the lower the quality of those signals. Looking at the previous example chart, we can see that if we bought or sold every time the price crossed the faster (5 period) average, we would be buying and selling almost every five minutes, and making lots of small losses.

The 30MA on the other hand (the dashed line) is crossed fewer times. The first couple of crosses would give us a just-about-profitable trade, the sell on the second cross being at a slightly higher price than the buy on the first cross. Around the middle of the chart it all goes a bit pear shaped though. The price zigzags up and down through the moving average on almost every bar. If we bought and sold on every one of those crosses we would quickly wipe out the small early profit and be into a losing situation.

Clearly then, just using the price crossing the moving average is not a good enough signal for trading. We need to filter it somehow, to stack up the odds more in our favour. We can do that by combining signals. For example, we could decide to trade price crosses only when they occur in the same direction as the overall trend. Because we are keeping an eye on the bigger picture, we should have a good idea of what that trend is. Indeed, we can use the moving average itself to tell us. In our example chart, the longer 30MA is trending downwards. So we could decide to trade only when the price crosses *below* that line, therefore trading with the trend instead of against it. That cuts down the number of trades, but still sees us making a lot of losing trades in that difficult middle area.

A better system would be rather than to use the price crossing the moving average as a trade signal, to use one moving average crossing another moving average as the signal. In doing so, we are using summary (bigger picture) information to base our decisions on. We're cutting out the detail and looking more at the overall trends. If we used the 5MA and 30MA of the previous chart, and used the points where they cross as trade signals, we would end up buying and selling on the points marked here:

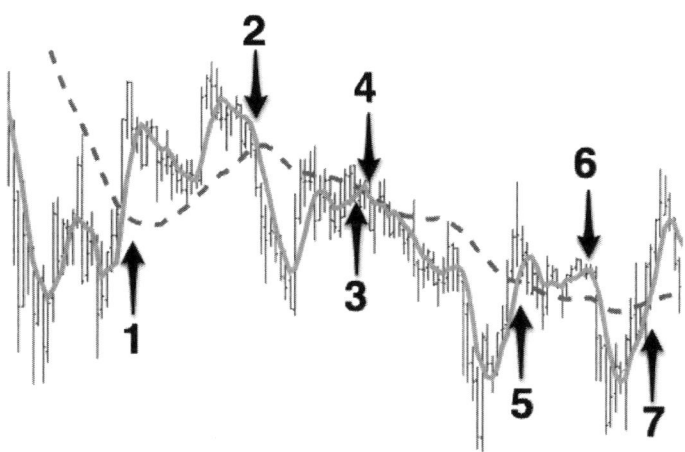

At point 1 we would buy, selling back again at point 2, for a very small profit. Another trade occurs between points 3 and 4, this time for a loss. Then there's another trade between points 5 and 6, which is another small loss. Finally we would enter a new trade at point 7, and as the chart ends there we don't know how that would pan out. In this example, we would have completed three trades, two of which would have been losers. Maybe in another chart they would all have been winners. To find out, we would need to test our system on lots of old charts to see how it works out over the long term. Testing like this is called *backtesting*, and is essential when developing trading strategies. We don't want to come up with an idea for a strategy and then just blindly trade it without knowing if it has a chance of success. Certainly we cannot base any decision about the viability of a system from a single chart segment like this, we need to see how it performs in all sorts of scenarios, on days where there is a lot

75

of activity and days where there is very little. The more old charts we can use when backtesting, the more confidence we can have in the potential of our system.

Returning to our example chart, we can refine our strategy further in the same way we refined the earlier strategy of using price crossing the moving average. That is to say we can choose to trade only the crosses which occur in the direction of the overall trend. We know that the trend here is downwards (as shown by the dashed 30MA), so here we would only trade when the 5MA crossed *below* the 30MA. This means we would sell short at point 2 on the chart, covering our position at point 3 when the 5MA briefly crossed above the 30MA. That would give us a small profit. We would almost immediately sell short again at point 4, covering our position at point 5. Another profitable trade. Our final trade would be to sell short at point 6, and cover at point 7, for about break even. Using this method we would have two profitable trades and one break even, considerably better than if we had traded every price cross.

So trading when one moving average crosses another, and doing so only when that happens in the direction of the trend, gives us a basic strategy that shows some promise. Even so, we can still do better. The trade selling short at point 2 and covering at point 3 only produces a small profit, because there's not much difference in the price between those two points, as highlighted in the circles:

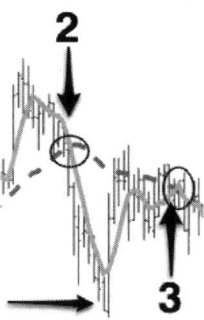

Yet at one point the price fell much lower, as highlighted by the sideways arrow above. When the price was that low, we would have had a very nice *unrealised* profit. Waiting until the MA crossed back at point 3 meant that this profit simply evaporated into thin air. Perhaps then, we could use the moving average crosses (in the direction of the overall trend) as a signal for *entering* our trades, and use a different signal for exiting, locking in more of the profit that was available. Later on, we'll explore some different ways to do exactly that. For now though, let's continue our exploration of moving averages, because they still have a few more tricks up their sleeve.

Variations On A Theme

So far the moving averages we've looked at have been the most simple kind. In fact they are actually called *simple moving averages* (the mathematics geniuses who create indicators aren't generally known for their creativity in naming things!) They are not the only kind of moving average though, they have some more exotic siblings. The most commonly used of these is the *exponential moving average*, or EMA. An EMA is calculated in almost the same way as a regular simple moving average (which we'll abbreviate as SMA), except that more weight is given to more recent bars. The idea is that recent price bars are more important than older price bars, so an EMA gives these recent bars a greater precedence in the calculation. The calculation for an EMA is done as follows:

Step 1: Start by calculating a simple moving average. To make things easier, we'll use the variety based on *last* prices. Given the following ten last prices:

$$1.12, 1.13, 1.12, 1.14, 1.15, 1.14, 1.15, 1.16, 1.17, 1.16$$

the 10 period simple moving average value for the current bar will be 1.14 (the sum of those last prices divided by ten).

Step 2: Calculate the *exponent* used to weight the EMA. The formula for this is:

$$\text{Exponent} = 2 \ / \ (\text{periods}+1)$$

So as we're calculating a 10 period EMA, the formula is $2/(10+1)$ which gives an exponent of 0.18

Step 3: Calculate the current bar's EMA value using the following formula:

$$\text{EMA} = (\text{close x exponent}) + (\text{previous bars EMA} \times (1 - \text{exponent}))$$

Clearly we need to know the previous bar's EMA value in order to calculate the current bar's value, and to know the previous bar's value, we need to know the value for the bar before *that*! In fact, given a 10 period EMA, we need a full 20 bars worth of data before we can get our first accurate EMA figure.

Don't worry, you'll never have to do this kind of calculation yourself, the charting software does it all for you. Charting software has access to plenty of historical data, so it can look back far enough to be able to calculate an accurate EMA for any chart you wish to view. I include the EMA calculation here because as with everything in trading, the better you understand how something works, the better use you can make of it.

Enough theory, let's take a look at an EMA alongside an SMA of the same period, so we can see the weighting effect in action:

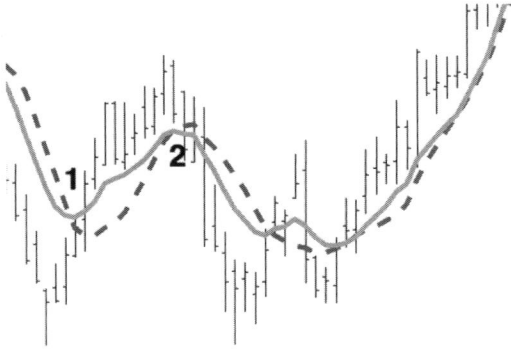

In this chart the dashed line is a 10 period simple moving average, and the solid line is a 10 period exponential moving average. Notice how the EMA more closely follows the movement of the price. At points 1 and 2 it turns to follow the price much more quickly than the SMA, which takes its time, meandering around, slowly catching up.

At this point you may be wondering which is better. There's no simple answer to that, both have advantages and disadvantages, just as there are advantages and disadvantages to using moving averages of different periods. The EMA is quicker to react, which means if we use it as a way of generating trading signals it will get us into trades earlier. On the other hand, if the price is just having a minor wobble, an SMA will give a better signal because it will filter that wobble out. Which we use then, depends on what we want to use them for. They are both tools in our trader's toolbox, and we should use them according to the situation.

Other Weighted Moving Averages

EMAs are the most common weighted moving average, but there are all sorts of other calculations available. More simplified versions apply constant weightings to earlier bars, rather than exponential weightings. Another variety uses *volume* to weight the moving average. Volume is the measure of quantity traded during a specific period. So if one five minute bar sees twice as much trading activity as the subsequent bar, a volume weighted moving average would give that bar double the weighting of the subsequent bar. This can be very useful when trading exchange traded instruments like stocks or futures, where we have an accurate figure for the volume being traded. As forex is not traded through a central exchange, we have no true idea of what kind of volume is being traded, and so volume weighted averages are far less useful to us.

Offset Averages

An alternative way of using moving averages is to *offset* them on the chart. Normally the MA is calculated up to the most recent bar, and that value is plotted in real time on the chart. It doesn't have to be done this way, many charting programs will allow us to calculate the MA in real time, but plot it a number of bars back. Here's what that looks like:

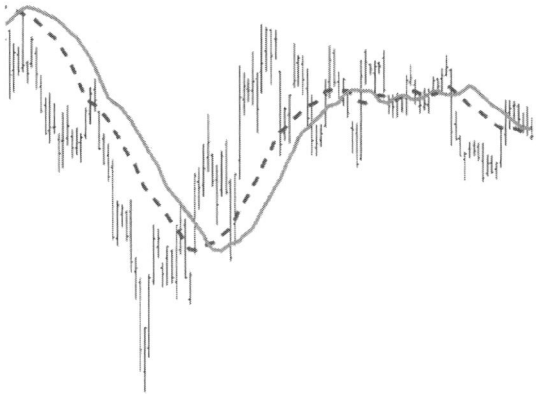

In this chart the dashed line is a 20 period SMA, and the solid line is the exact same SMA offset by 5 bars. It's a 5 bar old moving average! Offset MAs can be used as a basis for a trading strategy involving one MA crossing another. A glance at this example shows that entering trades when the real time MA crosses the offset (old) MA could provide useful trade entry signals.

Moving Average Envelopes

We can make an *envelope channel* out of a moving average, by adding a percentage value to the MA and plotting it above the MA line, and subtracting the same percentage value from the MA and plotting that below. Here's what that looks like on the chart:

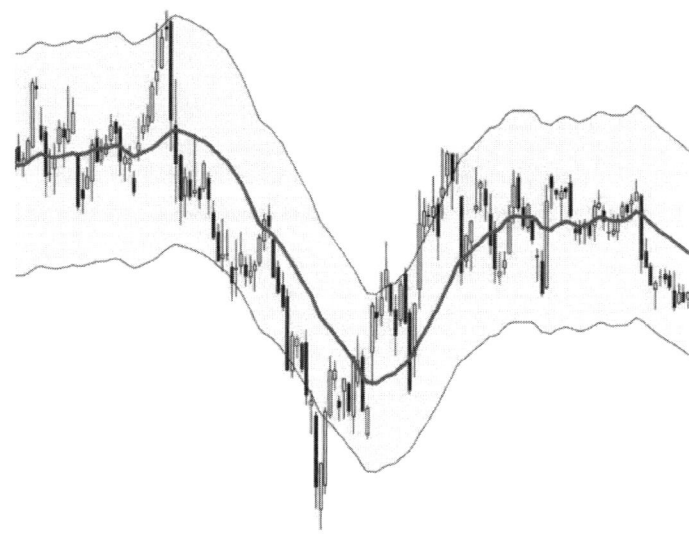

The central thicker line is a 20 period simple moving average. Above and below, the lines are the MA value plus and minus 10%. These bands create a *channel* which encompasses much of the price action.

The idea behind plotting this on a chart is to easily spot when the price moves a long way from the moving average. If the price moves outside the channel (the shaded area on this example chart) then the suggestion is that it has moved too far too quickly, and is due a correction. Either it will move sideways, allowing the moving average (and thus the channel) to catch up, or it will come back towards the moving average, and therefore back inside the channel. If this happens regularly, we could use such excursions outside the channel as possible signals to enter trades.

Commodity Channel Index

The commodity channel index (or CCI) is a different type of indicator, but is based very much on the moving average. It can be used in the same sort of way as the moving average envelope channel in the previous chart, by highlighting when the price moves a considerable distance from the average and is due a correction.

Let's see an example of CCI and it will be easier to make the link the MA:

Here we have another 5 minute chart, with a 20 period simple moving average applied. In the bottom part of the chart is the commodity channel index, or CCI. I've included a grid on this chart to make it easier to see the relationship between the price, the SMA, and the CCI. The CCI line has also been calculated using 20 periods. What it is effectively telling us is the relative movement between the price and the 20 period moving average. When the price is at the same point as the MA, the CCI is at zero (the 0 line is the middle line as indicated by the arrow). This can clearly be seen in the three highlighted areas on the chart. As the price moves away from its MA, so the CCI moves away from zero. Typically, when the CCI crosses +100 or −100, the price is considered over extended and a correction may be due. Simply watching the CCI criss-crossing the zero line doesn't tell us much more than watching the price relative to the moving average directly. However, the CCI has an interesting ability to forewarn of future changes in price trend. Let's zoom in on the second half of that chart and we'll see just such a forewarning:

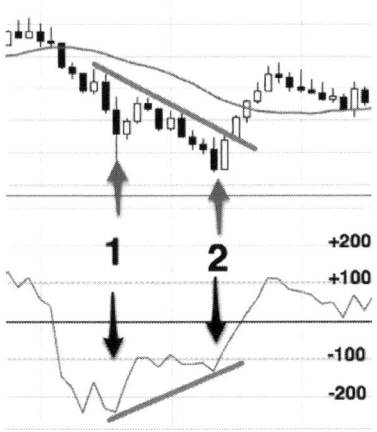

As we saw in the previous chart example, the overall trend for the price was downwards, the moving average showed that clearly. This portion of the chart shows that the trend may be about to change. The price is still in a down trend, which I've drawn on here. The low at point 2 is lower than that at point 1, which is what we expect in a down trend. However, the CCI is telling us something different; *its* low at point 2 is *higher* than its low at point 1. The CCI is in an up trend. When price and CCI differ like this, we call it *divergence*. The CCI trend is diverging from the price trend. Such divergence often precedes a change in trend, and indeed we can see that after the low at point 2, the price begins to rise. As the moving average begins to turn upwards, it becomes *support* for the price, the price bounces off. We can see this same information on the CCI when it bounces off the zero line.

Because of this ability to signal changes in trend ahead of time, we call the CCI a *leading indicator*. It can be a powerful tool as part of a trading strategy. For example, we could have a strategy whereby we look for these divergences, and when they occur, we enter a trade as the price breaks above its down trend line, or if we wanted to be more conservative, when it breaks above the moving average. Such a strategy combines two signals, the CCI / price divergence, and a break above the moving average or trend line. Remember, a combination of signals pointing us in the same direction is always preferable to a single signal. It provides us with confirmation, each signal backs up the other.

Relative Strength Index

The CCI is called an *oscillator*, because it oscillates around the zero line. Another very popular indicator is the relative strength index, or RSI, which oscillates between values of 0 and 100. The RSI is more about measuring the momentum of price changes—the speed at which changes occur. In use, the RSI is very similar to the CCI. It too, signals overextended prices, with values above 70 or below 30 considered as overbought and oversold, and a correction likely. That correction may simply be the price moving sideways for a while.

Another similarity the RSI shares with the CCI is its ability to predict trend changes through divergence, although these do tend to be clearer and earlier on the CCI. Here's an example chart showing both CCI and RSI:

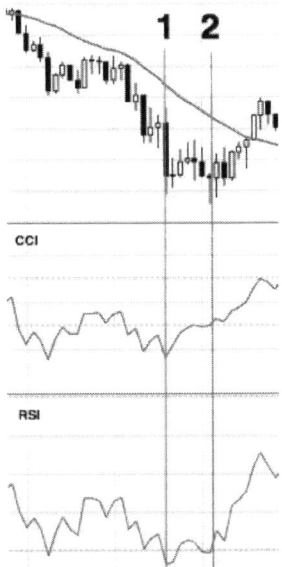

Here we see the price making lower lows in a down trend. The last two lows are labelled 1 and 2. Both the CCI and the RSI make a higher low at point 2, causing divergence. However, the divergence is much more pronounced on the CCI.

MISSION: Load up some more free forex charts, and add moving averages, as well as CCI and RSI to them. Play around with the values, seeing the effects of changing from simple to exponential moving averages. Try changing the number of periods in the calculation, and mixing and matching multiple MAs on the same chart. Do the same thing with CCI and RSI. Change their values and see how they look. Try finding divergences between the oscillators and the price. As a final exercise, try drawing trend lines, support, resistance, and triangle patterns on the CCI and RSI instead of on the price.

Indicators Summary

I've only touched on three indicators here, there are many more available. However, these three are the most commonly used, and as our goal is to see what other traders are seeing, we should concentrate our efforts on those indicators used by the majority.

Of course, there's no point using common indicators if we use uncommon settings to plot them. Popular values for moving averages are 10 period, 20 period, 34 period, and 50 period. When day trading, there is little to be gained by using values greater than 50. If you decide to trade over longer timeframes, then 100 and 200 period averages are also very common.

As far as the CCI is concerned, often used values are 14 and 20. Day traders looking to take very short term trades also sometimes use a 7 period CCI. The default and most common value for the RSI is 14 periods, but 20 periods is frequently plotted too.

When using these indicators, remember that they are all calculated from the price. That means there is nothing they can tell you that the price itself isn't already telling you. They are not a magic bullet with the power to predict the future. They are simply a way of summarising lots of information into an easy to read line on a chart. They can be very useful in providing confirmation of what the price itself is saying, but it would be dangerous to rely on them without reading the price at the same time.

Of the three indictors I have presented here, by far the most useful is the moving average. It offers a quick overview of what the price is doing. A flat moving average is quick confirmation that there is no trend, and that means a good time to stay out of the market. A steeply sloping moving average on the other hand, signals a strong trend, even if the individual price bars are whipping up and down making that trend less clear. One of the greatest uses of moving averages is to spot support and resistance. So many traders use them, they become self fulfilling. You will often see the price bounce off a common moving average.

Time Zones

One of the great things about the currency market is that it is traded the world over. The lack of a central exchange, and trading activity in almost every country on the planet, means the market is accessible 24/7 during the week. Even so, the market is much more active at certain times of day than others, namely, at the start of trading in each major time zone. There are three primary centres in the world for trading currency: New York in the USA, London in the UK, and Tokyo in Japan. To a lesser extent, Frankfurt in Germany and Sydney in Australia are also big players in the forex world. Trading hours in these markets are as follows:

Frankfurt 02:00 – 10:00 EST
London 03:00 – 11:00 EST
New York: 08:00 – 16:00 EST
Sydney 18:00 – 02:00 EST
Tokyo 19:00 – 15:00 EST

(See the Resources page on the website for a link to view these hours in your time zone.)

Nothing is stopping anyone from those countries trading forex outside those hours, these are simply "official" hours during which banks and institutions in each country are trading. As those banks and institutions make up the vast majority of the volume being traded, to all intents and purposes these are the effective trading hours in each region.

As day traders we are looking to enter and exit our trades the same day, so it makes sense for us to be looking at the market during a time when there is plenty of activity. There is little point in sitting down with a cup of coffee and a chart at 16:30 EST, because all the big players in the USA have packed up and gone home, everyone in Europe has been at home for hours, and those folks in Australia and Japan are barely out of bed yet. There's not going to be much in the way of action on the chart, prices will most likely be drifting sideways. We are much better off concentrating our efforts on the first hour or two of the market hours in one of the big three time zones—London, New York, or Tokyo. Which you choose will depend on personal circumstances. If you live in the UK and have a day job, you may well want to trade the open of Sydney and Tokyo at 11pm and midnight, London time. If you are a full time worker on the East Coast of America, then Sydney and Tokyo are available to you as well, opening at 6pm and 7pm Eastern time. Traders in Australia can try and be home in time to catch the London open at 5pm Sydney time. Of course, if you can be at home during the day, you have even more options.

What makes these opening hours in each time zone so great to trade? There's a lot of pent up energy that gets released when trading begins. The news cycle is 24 hours, and a lot can happen overnight. When traders come in to work in the morning, events overnight may well have caused a big shift in the consensus view of value for a particular currency. As that view gets traded in the market, it can make for big shifts in price. The bulk of this trading occurs as soon as the market opens, making that first hour or two the most volatile. Clearly it is easier to try and capture a small part of a large price move, than it is to try and get a big part of a small move, as this chart segment shows:

The difference in price between points 1 and 2 on this chart is about 10 pips. The difference between point 3 and point 4 is nearer 30 pips. If we had a strategy that caught 30% of a given move, that strategy would net us around 3 pips from the first move, and around 10 pips from the second move. So the bigger move would make us three times as much, all for the same amount of effort. Hopefully this makes the decision about when to trade pretty easy to make. We can either sit around for hours trying to grab a few pips here and there from a chart that is doing very little, or we can turn up just before the action starts, grab a piece of it early on, and be done for the day.

If your schedule means you can't be around at the market open, the next best time is the last hour of any given session. That's the time when a lot of consolidation happens. Traders that have taken speculative positions need to close them out before they finish for the day. Any news that has come out during the day but which hasn't fully been traded into the price, will get taken into account before the banks shut up shop. And some traders will look at what they've bought or sold during the day, decide they went further than they should have, and will look to offload their surplus (or indeed increase their position if they decide they were too conservative during the day). All this clearing up can make for some very nice moves in the last hour or so.

As a final note on time zones, it is worth favouring currency pairs related to the time zone you are trading. If you decide to trade the London open, regardless of your own location in the world, pairs including Sterling (GBP) would be preferable to pairs which would be completely foreign to London based traders. EUR/GBP would be better than CHF/AUD for example, as more London traders will be trading the former, meaning more volume and more action in that pair.

News

Earlier in the book we looked at how the currency market is particularly sensitive to the news cycle. Price perception is driven by news events and reports around the world, including:

Government borrowing and spending
Interest rate changes
Taxation
Credit ratings
Economic indicators
Civil unrest
Natural disasters

Most news happens without warning, so we can't very well use it as something on which to base decisions about potential future prices. However, economic indicators are a special subset of news. They don't just get put out there for all to see when the analyst compiling them has totted up the numbers, entered the last few figures on the spreadsheet, and printed out the final report. They are released at very specific times. For example, every month the US government releases the latest figures for the Consumer Price Index. This index is a measure of inflation, something that can have a considerable impact on the perception of currency value.

The day and time for the release of these figures is announced long before the figures themselves. Why? Because these kinds of numbers have the power to cause wild fluctuations in the prices of currencies, stocks, futures, and commodities. Knowing ahead of time when these important economic indicators are going to be announced allows market participants to prepare their positions accordingly. For the likes of you and me, that generally means getting out of the market altogether. The price swings brought about by indicators like the Consumer Price Index can be so violent, they have the potential to shift our positions into immediate and considerable loss.

These news driven price moves are a bit like a huge tidal wave hitting a surf beach. You could be a pretty good surfer, quite at home riding the waves, but when a massive tidal wave looms up out of nowhere, suddenly you are out of your depth and in serious danger of drowning. If you know that a tidal wave like that is due at exactly 9:30AM, the chances are you would get out of the water beforehand, probably with a few minutes to spare, just to be sure. From the safety of the beach you could then enjoy the spectacle of the wave as it hit, jumping back in to continue your surfing as soon as the water was a little more calm, maybe riding some of the turbulence caused by the passing wave (okay, I'm not a surfer, but you get the picture!)

The same applies to the release of programmed economic news. Such releases usually bring about a huge tidal wave of trading, causing prices to swing violently up and down unpredictably as market participants rush to try and interpret the numbers. Being out of the market at that time is the safest position to hold. Once things calm down a little and a direction appears to become established, there is still profit to be found in the aftershock.

Fortunately for us, we have ample warning of all these kinds of announcements. Any decent economic calendar will inform us of programmed news releases for the day, week, and sometimes even month ahead. As well as economic indicators, there may be government budget announcements, central bank interest rate decisions, economic reports, and prominent figures making speeches to worry about. Not every indicator or news event has the potential to be market moving, and good economic calendars will grade these events, giving an idea of the intensity of price movement they may cause. With experience, you yourself will come to get a feel for which announcements make things happen, and which pass by apparently unnoticed. For some links to economic calendars, check out the Resources page. I would highly recommend looking at two different calendars before every trading session. It has been known for events to get left off calendars in the past. The thirty seconds extra it takes each day to cross check two calendars is well worth it for the extra layer of security provided. Most traders who forget to check the calendar before trading, only ever forget once!

Interpretation Not Required

It can be tempting to join in the game and try to interpret economic indicators as they are released. Most of the major numbers have guidance published ahead of time. Teams of analysts and gurus will try and predict the figure, presumably to try and justify their highly paid jobs. This largely pointless exercise simply serves to whip up even more chaos once the actual number is released. Traders frantically try and work out *"Is it better than expected? Worse? The same…?"*

We might imagine that a number which comes out better than expected could cause prices to rise. But traders can be fickle, and big players could be expecting it to be even better than it actually was (despite the predictions and guidance), be disappointed, and initiate a sell-off causing prices to crash. The point is, nobody knows what is going to happen, and trying to make predictions is really no better than gambling. There's nothing to be gained by attempting it, and a lot to be lost. It is much safer, and more profitable, to let the big money move things around a bit, then jump in on their coat-tails once things have settled down. Later on, when we start looking at building a strategy in more detail, we will examine a couple of ways to do exactly this, profiting from news in relative safety.

Chapter Four

How To Trade

So far we've examined what makes the forex market tick. We've seen what price is and what makes it change. We've also seen how we can look at these changes historically, in the form of charts, and how those charts can give us clues about future price changes. Now it is time to see how to put all this knowledge to use and actually trade forex, the nuts and bolts of how to enter, manage, and exit our trades for maximum efficiency, and minimum risk. In this section we'll look at everything that is necessary to go from reading this book, to sitting in front of a screen, buying and selling currencies.

Brokers

As I mentioned earlier when we were first looking at the players in the forex market, *broker* isn't really the right word for the companies who enable the buying and selling of currencies for us retail traders. But it is pretty universally used, so we shall continue to use it here.

Broadly speaking there are two tiers of broker, wholesale and retail. Wholesale brokers are the big institutions who enable currency trading among the major players—the banks. These guys deal in huge numbers, enabling transactions worth trillions of Dollars every day. For their trouble, they take a modest fee for each transaction. As a percentage, their commissions are very low. For example, ICAP, one of the biggest brokers in the business, charges around $1 commission for every million Dollars traded. We can pretty much forget about them though, as unless we are planning on trading numbers which end with seven or eight zeros, they're not going to be interested in our business.

Retail brokers resell currency trading services to everyone else in the market, including mere mortals like you and me. When we transact with a retail broker, the transaction gets grouped with thousands of others and eventually passes through a wholesale broker further up the chain. In fact, buying and selling currency is very much like buying and selling any other commodity. Regular punters like us go into a shop (a retailer) to buy stuff, and that shop in turn gets its stock from a wholesaler. With currency, the retailer is the broker we deal with, and they in turn deal with wholesale brokers to transact large sums of currency between themselves, balancing their books and trying to make a profit at the same time.

Within the retail sector there are a number of different offers available. Most people who have been on vacation to a foreign land will have experience of using a bank or travel agency as a retail currency broker. You take your regular currency in (usually in the form of a credit card these days), and they exchange it for cash in the currency of the country you will be visiting. Sometimes they will charge a commission for this, sometimes not. Either way, they will make a good profit from your transaction because the exchange rate they offer will be vastly inferior to the wholesale rate, also called the *interbank rate*. For example, the interbank exchange rate between the British Pound Sterling and the Euro might be £1 = €1.211. The retail rate offered by a travel agency, airport, or bank on the other hand, will be around £1 = €1.182. That means if you wanted to change £200 into Euros for a weekend away in Paris, you would get €236.40 for your money. The bank on the other hand, can use your £200 to buy Euros through a wholesale broker at the better interbank rate. When they do so, they'll get €242.35 (£200 @ 1.211 Euros to the Pound). The end to end transaction has netted them a profit of €5.95, the difference between the Euros they bought at the interbank rate and what they sold you at the retail rate. Of course, they won't turn round and spend your £200 on Euros immediately. The Pounds Sterling funds will be pooled with those from other customers and lumped together into a much larger trade. And as they aren't daft, they won't execute that trade immediately; they have their own talented traders who will be watching the market, trying to time their trade to be as profitable as possible. The retail brokers are playing the same game as us, just on a bigger scale.

Banks, travel agents, and high street currency exchanges may well be easily accessible to us, but they are wholly unsuitable for forex day trading. They offer very uncompetitive exchange rates which would make it more difficult to trade profitably (large chunks of profit would be eaten up just covering the costs of these rates). They also take a considerable amount of time to execute trades (many minutes) time during which the market may have moved, and we would have lost out on valuable profit. The final nail in the coffin as far as these types of brokers is concerned is that they deal in cash. In order to buy a thousand Dollars worth of Japanese Yen, we would need to hand over a thousand Dollars. That might sound fair and reasonable, but there are much better offers out there which will allow us to carry out the same transaction using other people's money.

Alternative Instruments

As well as trading forex directly, we can trade through so-called derivative instruments. These are synthetic trading devices that are based on the price of currencies. The two best known are futures and CFDs. Both are contracts which in and of themselves have no intrinsic value. The value comes from what they represent. In the case of a futures contract, this represents an obligation to buy or sell a certain quantity of an underlying asset (in this case, currency) for a certain price, at a certain time in the future. In a CFD (or Contract For Difference), the contract exists purely as an abstraction of the underlying asset. In other words it is a proprietary contract whose price is fixed to follow the price of a certain currency. Without getting bogged down in details, these and other derivatives make it possible to trade based on the price of currencies without actually trading those currencies themselves. There are some reasons why this may be advantageous (particularly in the case of Spread Bet derivatives, a subset of CFDs, which have an attractive tax status in some jurisdictions), but for most people, plain simple forex with a regular broker is the way to go. Futures are more expensive to trade, and require a larger initial budget. CFDs can be cheap and easy, but as a proprietary instrument it is easy for the provider (the equivalent to a broker, but most certainly not a broker in the true sense) to manipulate prices. There is no advantage to trading them significant enough to make it worth doing so in favour of regular forex.

Trading With Other People's Money

It may sound crazy, but it is entirely possible, easy in fact, to trade using the funds of other people. People we have never met, and are never likely to meet, are quite happy to make their money available for us to trade with. These people are the last category of broker—the retail brokers who are specifically set up to cater to the needs of speculative currency traders like us.

Now found almost exclusively online, these brokers introduce a whole different model for trading currencies. For the sake of simplicity, and for lack of a better name, from here on I'll simply refer to brokers of this variety as *online forex brokers* or *internet brokers*. Generic I know, but these are the guys we are going to be working with day in day out. We can discount all the other types, as far as we're concerned online forex brokers are the entities who make day trading currencies possible.

Online forex brokers work in a totally different way to all the other kinds. Instead of stumping up cash for each and every transaction, we start by depositing cash into a trading account. This account will be denominated in a base currency, usually US Dollars, British Pounds Sterling, or Euros. The minimum deposit varies from broker to broker. Many internet brokers now accept deposits as low as $25, although such a small amount severely limits the trading that can be done and therefore the utility of the account. A more reasonable starting balance would be around $200 or equivalent in another base currency.

Placing trades is done using the brokers internet interface, clicking buttons on their secure website. When we come to buy some currency, part of the price of that currency is deducted from our account balance by way of payment. The rest of the payment is put up by the broker. They lend us the money to complete the transaction. How much they lend depends on the broker, but it can be 95% or more!

Let's look at an example. We'll imagine that we want to buy some Swiss Francs. We decide to buy a thousand US Dollars worth. When we click the order button, instead of $1000 being deducted from our account, only $50 is taken. The other $950 is put up by the broker. The cash that we put in is called *margin*. Trading this way allows us to control much greater amounts of currency than we could possibly buy using our own funds. As soon as the order executes, our account is credited with the appropriate quantity of Swiss Francs, and we are said to be *long* Swiss Francs. At some point we must close the trade by selling those Francs back in return for Dollars. When that sale occurs, $950 from the proceeds is returned to the broker, and we get whatever is left. If the value of the Swiss Franc had risen against the Dollar, and we sold ours back for $1200, the broker would take their $950 and we would end up with $250 being credited back to our balance, a profit of $200. That's a nice return of 20% on the $1000 transaction, and an even more impressive 400% return on the $50 of our own money that we put up.

If things had gone the other way though, matters become more complicated. As soon as our position moved into loss (the Swiss Franc lost value against the Dollar), the broker would need to take a little more margin from our account balance, to ensure that they were going to get all their money back when we closed the position. If things went so far against us that we had no more money in the account to cover the margin required by the broker, they would automatically close out our position, keeping the proceeds to cover the cash they had lent us for the trade, and leaving our account empty.

The credit offered to us by the broker doesn't come for free. If we choose to keep our trade open overnight, they will charge us interest. At the same time, we would earn interest on the Swiss Franc balance in our account, and things would pretty much equal themselves out. As day traders this is something we'll never likely experience as we never hold overnight, but if you choose to do so it's worth checking with your broker exactly how their margin interest works.

So far so good, but what happens if instead of buying Swiss Francs against the US Dollar we decide we want to trade them against the Euro? Our account is funded with Dollars, we don't have any Euros to trade with. No problem, whatever the base currency our broker account is denominated in, they will do the required conversion behind the scenes for us. We may have a US Dollar account, but that doesn't stop us buying the Swiss Franc against the Euro, or the Japanese Yen against Sterling, or indeed any other combination on offer. The margin requirement will be automatically converted to US Dollars and deducted from our account. When we come to sell back our position, any resulting profit will also be converted back to our US Dollar base currency. Indeed even throughout the trade as the prices move, we'll be shown our *unrealised* profit or loss in our own base currency (unrealised profit or loss is that which would occur if we exited our position right now, but as yet is only theoretical as the position is still open).

Enough with the explanation, let's make this all a bit more real by looking at an actual order ticket and see how it relates to these concepts. For our example, we'll imagine we are trading AUD/CAD—the Australian Dollar against the Canadian Dollar. Our broker is offering the following prices:

The ask price is 1.03322, which means they will sell us 1.03322 Canadian Dollars for one Australian Dollar. The bid price is 1.03296, which means they will buy 1.03296 Canadian Dollars for one Australian Dollar. The difference between these two figures is 2.6, which means we have a *spread* of 2.6 pips. If we buy Canadian Dollars for Australian Dollars, we need those Canadian Dollars to appreciate in value by 0.00026 before we can sell them back at break even. If they appreciate by any more than that, we'll make a profit. We decide to buy Canadian Dollars against Aussie Dollars, here's what our order ticket might look like:

The first thing we notice is that this is a *buy* order. We are buying Canadian Dollars with Australian Dollars. The *Units* number refers to the number of those Canadian Dollars we are buying. In this ticket, we have entered 1000. The quote confirms the price per Canadian Dollar, so we can see if it changes right up to the second we hit the button. After that there are some boxes we don't need to worry about for now, and at the bottom of the ticket we see some numbers which explain this order in monetary terms. The Units Available is the number of Canadian Dollars the broker has available for sale—more than enough for our little trade! The next line shows the value of a 1 pip price move given the number of units we are trading. In this case, as we are trading 1000 units, every 1 pip the price moves in our favour is worth 0.10 US Dollars to us (the value is in US Dollars because that's the base currency of this account). The Trade Value is the cost of this trade when converted to US Dollars. In this case, $1031.31. Finally the Margin Used tells us that the broker will be taking $51.57 (US Dollars) from our account, our *margin* requirement, and they will pay the rest.

If we click the confirm button to enter this order, assuming it executes as shown, we will be buying a thousand Canadian Dollars at a rate of 1.03322 per Australian Dollar, but we'll be paying for the transaction in US Dollars! This can all get a little confusing, but with practice it becomes easy to not think about the various currency exchanges going on in the background, and simply see the price of the pair we are trading.

To make things easier, rather than thinking about buying one currency with another, via a third, we can instead think of the currency pair being traded as an entity—a thing—in its own right. So instead of thinking in terms of buying Canadian Dollars for Australian Dollars, paid with US Dollars, we can simply think of buying 1000 "AUD/CAD"s for 1.03322, just like we might buy 1 "loaf of bread". When it comes time to sell, we can sell our 1000 "AUD/CAD"s for whatever bid price the broker is offering. That is not to say we should divorce ourselves entirely from the fact that what we are trading are the currencies of two large countries. We always need to bear in mind the mechanics of these currencies and what makes them move. But once it comes to executing trades, thinking of pairs as generic things that we can buy and sell makes life easier.

Margin Can Be Dangerous

Trading with other people's money, or trading on margin, opens up much greater potential profits than we could hope to achieve if we had to pay outright for every trade we made. As we've seen, trading 1000 units of AUD/CAD yields a return of only 10 US Dollar cents for every one pip movement in the price. If we want to make some decent money, either that price is going to have to move a massive amount, or we need to increase our trade size. We can't force the price to move, but increasing size is something within our control. If we bought 100,000 units, each pip's movement would then be worth about $10 US Dollars, much more interesting. Without margin, a trade of that size would cost us over a hundred thousand US Dollars, putting it well out of the reach of most traders. But with margin, we need put up only around five thousand Dollars, the broker pays the rest.

This all sounds wonderful, but behind those attractive potential profits lurk equally sizeable potential losses. Just as a trade of 100,000 units can *earn* us $10 a pip if things go our way, so it can *lose* us $10 a pip if they don't. Prices can move fast, running up substantial losses in minutes. We may only put up a fraction of the cash required for the trade, but we are, naturally, fully liable for any losses. Those losses, like any potential profits, can become greatly disproportionate to the size of our account. Margin is a powerful tool, an essential one almost, but like any powerful tool it must be treated with respect as used incorrectly it can do massive damage to a trading account.

Choosing A Broker

Now we understand what a powerful and essential tool margin is, we can better appreciate why high street foreign exchange shops and retail banks aren't going to cut the mustard. We need a specialist broker who offers margin, rapid order entry and exit, and access to all of this through a slick online interface. Fortunately for us, the popularity of forex trading means that there are literally hundreds of brokers like this around.

I'm not going to single out any one broker here and recommend it to you. Partly that's because if I did so, Sod's Law says that as soon as this book is published that broker will either go into administration, radically change their business, or turn into the worst customer service experience known to mankind. Rather than inflict such a future on any poor undeserving business, I will give you some advice on how to pick a broker for yourself.

Picking a broker is a little like choosing a car. They all do the same basic job, but their strengths may well lay in different areas. What appeals to you in a particular broker, may well be the kiss of death for another trader. I recommend you draw up a list of attributes you require, then hop onto your preferred search engine, type in "forex brokers", and settle down with a good cup of coffee and work your way through the results to see who appeals to you.

The main criteria you will be interested in should be:

— The countries they accept customers from. Forex might be a worldwide market, but regulation happens at a national level. Sadly the USA has particularly onerous trading regulations which mean that a large number of discount brokers simply do not accept customers from the States.

— The minimum deposit. There's no point signing up with a broker who requires that you place $2000 in your account if you only have $150 to your name.

— Base currencies accepted. You need to be able to deposit and withdraw funds from your account, and that's done using a base currency. If your own currency is the US Dollar, Sterling, or the Euro, most brokers will be happy to take your money. Outside of those and things can get a little more complicated. This links to the next item:

— Deposit methods. You need to get money into your broker account to trade with. If your chosen broker accepts deposits via credit card then you can send funds in their preferred base currency and your card provider will convert them to your own currency. That gets round the base currency problem if you're own currency isn't supported by the broker, but be aware that your credit card company will not make the conversion at the interbank rate, it will be a rate far more favourable to themselves! Aside from credit cards, other deposit options include wire transfers (which tend to be quite country specific), PayPal, and Western Union. A lot of smaller brokers will also accept eGold or even Bitcoin. I personally don't recommend using either of these as they are not government backed or regulated currencies. Who knows if they will disappear overnight, taking your deposit with them?

— Withdrawal methods. Funding your account is only half the story. Once you have accumulated some profit, you will want to get it out of the broker account and into your bank account. Wire transfers are preferable (no cheques to get lost in the post), but these can get very expensive when they cross international borders. PayPal is easy and fairly ubiquitous. Some brokers offer their own prepaid credit card and will load your profits onto that for you to spend as you wish.

— Currency pairs available. It almost goes without saying that you will want to be sure your broker offers the currency pair(s) you are hoping to trade.

— Company health / Backing. Who is behind the brokerage? Is it a multinational publicly traded company, or a bunch of kids running a white label operation out of a garage or bedroom? How long have they been around? Do they have published accounts? Are they in debt and liable to disappear, taking your hard earned profits with them? When you're depositing money with any company, do your homework and make sure you know who you're dealing with.

— Regulation. Depending on where in the world you live, and where in the world the broker is based, you, they, or both, may be subject to regulation. It is your responsibility to find out what applies in your situation and abide by it.

— Accreditation. Badges of honour and accreditations posted on brokers' websites look pretty, but do they mean anything? Don't choose a broker just because they won some arbitrary award, check it out and make sure it's not a made up badge designed as a clever marketing ploy.

— Trading platform / Charts. Forex charts don't need to be fancy, quite the opposite. But they do need to be easy to use, real time, and reliable. The same goes for the trading platform, the software you use to enter orders and manage trades. The choice of platform and charts is very much a personal one, so take the time to try what's on offer from your short list of brokers. Every broker worth their salt offers a free trial account—use it! Put the software and the broker through their paces. These are your tools of the trade, and you need to be sure you are going to get along with them. The time to find that out is in a demo or practice account, not in a live account as you try and make your first few trades with real money on the line.

— Customer service. I would highly recommend talking to your short listed brokers before opening any account. Are they easy to get hold of? Can you email them? Call them? Get them on Twitter or Skype? Do they have a physical presence so that if things go bad you can walk into their office and have it out with them? When you do talk to them, how do they respond? Are they knowledgable about their product and the world of forex? Do they want to help, or are they just there to fob you off and refer you to the FAQ page? Your broker is your partner in your forex career, you will be working with them every day. As you narrow down your list and speak with a few, treat it like a job interview.

All this sounds like a lot, and it might also sound like I'm suggesting that most brokers are scoundrels, out to scam you for all they can. That's not the case. Most brokers are decent honest firms, doing their best to provide a great service. You just need to use common sense when choosing who you are going to work with. If you were looking to open a new bank account, the chances are you wouldn't search Google and open an account with the first bank on the list, regardless of whether or not you had heard of them. You would check them out a little, make sure they are legitimate and likely to be around for the long term. And you'd probably speak to a few friends or colleagues to see if anyone had any experience of them. The same goes for a broker. Don't blindly send off your cash to the first pretty looking website you see, anyone can whip up one of those. At the same time, don't worry too much about finding the perfect broker first time. Changing broker isn't as painful as changing bank, you can open another account, plop some funds in there and away you go. The biggest hurdle to overcome if you wanted to change broker down the line, would be learning a new trading interface.

The Trading Environment

With your broker account open and funded, you will be ready to trade. The broker will have provided you with a trading platform, including charts and a way of entering your buy and sell orders. It may be proprietary or it may be a package that works with multiple brokers. Either way, you'll want to take the time to get to know it. This is your day to day work environment, your tools of the trade. You need to be able to find your way round the interface, to be able to make it do what you want without having to think about it. As I mentioned earlier, a demo account is invaluable for this. A practice trading account is like a flight simulator to an airline pilot. It lets you push buttons, scroll windows, mess things up, and try things out all in total safety. Once you're ready to "go live", you will be able to focus all your attention on what matters most—your analysis of the market and your management of the trades you are making. The interface should melt away into the background, quietly carrying out your bidding.

Trading platforms vary in their details, but as a minimum they will all present you the following essential elements:

Charts. Your most important tool, the one you will spend most of your time looking at. Take a moment to explore the different display options on offer. Choose whether you want to use bar charts or candlesticks. Play around with the colours, of both the bars and the background. See what is easy on your eye and clear and simple to read. Try changing the size of the bars, find a good compromise between clarity and fitting enough information on the screen. Set up any indicators you will be using. When you have your chart the way you want it, make sure to save the settings! It's a terrible sinking feeling when after half an hour of tweaking, you lose the lot.

Account overview. This window tells you how much cash you have to trade with. When you have a position (or positions) open, it will inform you of the state of your margin—your buying power.

Order ticket. The ticket is how you send buy and sell orders to the broker. We will look at the different order types and their uses in a moment. Many platforms let you to configure your default order ticket. So for example you may be able to set up a default order size, and an automatic stop to be sent with every order. There may even be the possibility to set up one-click order buttons that instantly send a buy or sell order for a fixed amount of whatever you have on your chart at a given moment, saving valuable seconds between making the decision and getting the order in.

Order history. This area shows your currently open orders as well as previous orders. Obviously you will want this to feature somewhere prominently on your screen. Opening a position then forgetting about it until you open your account the next morning isn't a great feeling! Keep track of what you are doing in the order history or management section.

In addition to these, you should have the following windows easily at hand for each trading session:

Economic Calendar. To remind you of those all important news releases that will be happening during the day. I would highly recommend using some kind of automatic alert system that can prod you with a beep and perhaps a flashing warning message a few minutes before each of these. It's all well and good reading the calendar before you start trading, but when you're absorbed in watching a beautiful pattern emerge on the chart, it can be very easy to forget about the jobless figures about to be announced. There are lots of free alert programs for Windows and Mac computers, and these days most mobile phones have several ways to set up noisy reminders as well.

Live news feed. Your calendar will tell you about news that we know about in advance, but news has a funny habit of happening all the time, without warning. A terrorist attack, or major earthquake, or any number of other events can and will happen while you are trading, and they can have a major impact on prices. If you are in a trade when something happens, the chances are you'll see it on your chart long before it hits a newsfeed, and you'll have to manage it accordingly. But, and I know I risk sounding mercenary here, if you do catch something on the news and you're not in a trade, that news item can be an alert to a potential opportunity. On a more general level, we are always trying to build a view of the overall market sentiment, where the price is headed in the bigger picture. Being aware of what is happening in the world is part of the process of building that view. Your news feed could be a 24 hour news channel, but they are slow by today's standards. Better to use a web feed (see the Resources page for some ideas). Even better is Twitter. It's often dismissed as a means for celebs to inform their fans about what they had for breakfast, but in reality it is the fastest news channel currently out there.

Trading journal. We'll be looking later at why recording some quick details about every trade you take is essential to your success. I recommend that you do this longhand on paper, but if you really can't stand to use a pen, then some kind of note taking program is better than not doing it at all.

Hardware

All of these programs need to run on some kind of machine. Any recent computer is fine, as long as it is reliable, and not infested with spyware, adware, or any other form of malware. Whether you choose to use a Mac or a Windows computer, keep it up to date with the latest security patches and a good antivirus. When trading, close down everything that is not directly related to what you're doing. Kill your iTunes, shut down the email, and quit any games. This is as much for your benefit as it is for the machine. You will both perform better if you are focussed solely on the job in hand—managing your trades. I'm not going to make any recommendation here about screen size, memory or hard drive capacity, or the speed of your CPU. The fact is that almost any regular computer purchased in the last few years should be more than capable of running a forex trading setup (with the exception of very cheap netbooks, which are underpowered and should not be considered, and tablets, which don't have the breadth of software, yet). Everything else is down to personal choice. Certainly you don't need fifteen monitors, one is perfectly sufficient. I do have a preference for trading from a laptop simply because the battery makes for good backup if the power goes off mid-trade, but that's only useful if you still have a connection to the internet, which brings us to connectivity.

For your internet connection, I recommend getting the fastest available and within your budget. Trading data is tiny relative to HD YouTube videos and the like, but faster connections usually have lower latency, which means your order gets to the broker quicker when you click the button. Seconds can make a difference to your bottom line in a fast moving market, so skimping on your internet connection is a false economy. Dial-up connections still exist in some parts of the world, and are really not suitable for trading, they're simply too slow and unreliable. Satellite connections suffer from terrible latency and are also unsuitable. Regular wired broadband connections (DSL) are best, be they copper or fibre. Wireless connections like WiMax, 3G, or 4G LTE are all ok if they have proven themselves to be reliable and you have a good strong signal. Piggybacking on the next door neighbour's WiFi is not so great!

If you have other people and computers in your household sharing the same connection, kick them off when you are trading. You don't want to find yourself in a losing trade, with money draining from your account as you repeatedly hit the sell button and nothing happens because Aunt Mabel has decided this is just the moment to settle down and watch that Susan Boyle clip for the sixty third time. If you are serious about trading to the point of making it a full time source of income, then it is well worth considering a second internet connection dedicated to your forex efforts. Again, it's one of the tools of the trade, and not something to economise on. One poorly executed order can easily cost you more than several months internet service and a new laptop combined.

Not essential but recommended is some form of power backup. Laptops, as I mentioned, have batteries which will keep them going if and when the lights go out. Your internet router won't be so lucky. An uninterruptible power supply (UPS) is a cheap device that provides battery power to whatever you plug into it. Using one with your router means that if the power does go off, you have at least a few minutes connectivity in which you can safely close any open positions. It is better to miss the opportunity to be making a profit, than to be in a trade you can't get out of and have that trade go bad.

Alternatively, mobile devices are getting better and better at providing connectivity without all those messy wires and mains power supplies. More and more forex brokers are offering iPhone and Android apps. This alone can be a good enough reason to go with a given broker. I don't suggest using those apps to trade from (they're too small and fiddly), but they can be a lifesaver for getting you out of a position if something happens to your trading computer.

As a final security measure, find out if your broker can take orders by telephone. If all else fails and you have a mobile phone handy (with the broker's number in the memory, naturally), you can call them up and get them to close out your position.

Currency Pairs

Internet forex brokers typically offer thirty or more different currency pairs to trade. We don't want to watch all of these. We only have a certain amount of attention that we can give to the charts in front of us, and the more pairs we try and follow, the thinner that attention will be spread. Too thin, and we'll miss great trades. So we should limit the number of pairs we watch. Initially, just two is enough. With more experience, keeping tabs on three or four is reasonable. It's certainly *possible* to watch more than that, but it is not desirable. If price is a language, then each currency pair is like a dialect. It has its own vocabulary, phrasing, and sound. It moves in a certain way, it has personality. The more time we spend studying a pair, the better we will get to know it. We will become accustomed to its quirks and habits. We will be able to subconsciously pick up on tiny signals that we've seen time and again, and they will give us added confidence in our trades. Becoming a specialist of one or two currency pairs is much easier that trying to become a specialist of four or five. We may have less opportunity when following just a couple of pairs, but that can be more than made up for by getting more from each trade, and from winning a higher percentage of trades.

Choosing Pairs

There are two simple criteria we can use to pick out the currency pairs we want to watch:

Timezone. A trader based in the USA and trading regular daytime hours has less interest in following the AUD/JPY than, say, the GBP/USD. Much of the trading of the former pair will, of course, be coming from Japan and Australia. All the action will be happening when the US based trader is away from the screen. It makes much more sense to trade a pair that is being traded in the same timezone the trader is in. So the first thing to decide is when you will be trading, then pick some pairs that are seeing most of their activity occurring in the same zone.

Volume & Volatility. I'm sure someone somewhere has a very good reason to be trading the ZAR/CZK, but they are in a minority. An exotic pair like that sees far fewer trades than a major pair like the EUR/USD or GBP/JPY. We need prices to move if we want to be able to make trades, and that movement comes from market activity, which we call volume (literally the number of trades taking place). Little point then, in watching pairs where nothing happens. We should concentrate our efforts where the action is—the major pairs. USD, GBP, EUR, and JPY are all major world currencies, and any combination makes a good pair to watch.

Entering Trades

You have your trading computer up and running, and are logged into your broker platform. You've been watching the chart and an opportunity to take a trade presents itself (more on that part in the strategy section). You pull up an order ticket and are presented with a number of options about how your order is presented. There are four main *order types* available: market orders, limit orders, stop orders, and stop limit orders. Each has its own unique merits, which we will examine now.

Market Order

This is the most simple kind of order. It says *"I want to buy (or sell) this pair, right now, whatever the price is."* The order gets to the broker and is matched with the first available order on the other side. So if it is a buy order, our order will be matched with the first available sell order. Our base currency is exchanged for the sellers quote currency at whatever the current price happens to be. When an order completes, we say it has been *filled*, and the price at which it happens is called the *fill price*. This fill price could be different to the price shown on the screen at the moment the order is sent, particularly in fast moving conditions. The market order doesn't care, it never looks at the price, it just gets the job done regardless. If your order executes at a price worse than that on offer at the instant you sent it, we call the difference *slippage*. Slippage can become quite a considerable cost, but there is a way we can eliminate it, using the next order type.

Limit Order

This is a little more involved. A limit order (sometimes called simply an "entry order" by some forex brokers) says *"I want to buy (or sell) this pair at a certain price or* better." The order is sent to the broker who will keep it open until someone comes along on the other side, ready to trade at the price we specified in the limit order (called the *limit price*) or a better price. *Better* in this case means better from our point of view. So if, for example, our order was for the USD/GBP pair and the current price was 0.6316 we might send a limit order to buy with a limit price of 0.6314. Our order would sit at the broker until the price dropped to our limit price or lower, at which point it would execute. Using limit orders then, eliminates slippage entirely. On the other hand, because they are strict about the price they execute at, limit orders may never get filled, the actual price may never reach the limit price. Even if the price does get there, limit orders are filled on a first-come first-served basis. If there are lots of other limit orders in front of ours in the queue, they will get executed first. By the time ours reaches the top of the queue, the price may well have moved back up, meaning we don't get a fill. A third possibility exists. If our order is very large, it may well get partially filled before the price moves away, stopping the order from completing entirely. For example, if we were trying to buy 100,000 EUR/USD, it is entirely possible that we end up buying 50,000 and then the price moves back up, preventing the other 50,000 from being purchased. *Partial fills* like this are very uncommon in forex as the volumes traded are huge, but they can happen.

Limit orders are perfect for entering new trades because we can essentially set the worst price at which we are willing to buy or sell. We know that if the order executes, it will be at that price or better. If we think the price is going up, we want to buy before that happens. If we use a market order, there's a possibility that some of the move upwards will already be over by the time our order gets filled, wiping out some of our potential profit before we even get started. If we use a limit order though, we can effectively say *"I want in, but I'm not paying more than x"*. If our order fills, we stand to profit from the entire move upwards, and if it doesn't, then it just saved us from getting hit by slippage.

So much for buying, what about selling? A limit order to sell requires the price to meet or exceed the limit price. So in our USD/GBP example, if the price was 0.6316 we might send a limit sell order with a limit price of 0.6318. Our order would execute if the price reached or exceeded 0.6318.

In both of these examples we have sent limit orders with prices *better* than the current price. In doing so, we are actually hoping for the price to move against us slightly before going the way we expect. In the case of the buy order, we presumably expect the price to rise, so asking to get in at a lower than current price means it has to drop first. We're trying to not only limit slippage, but to actually get a better entry price than is currently on the table. That carries a risk of not getting filled at all. A better way to use limit orders for entering new trades is rather than try and eliminate slippage, just restrict it. We can do that by sending a limit order with the limit price as the current price plus a couple of pips. Going back to our USD/GBP example, the price is currently 0.6316 and we think it's going to rise. A suitable order then, might be to send a limit buy with a limit price of 0.6318 (0.6316 current price + 2 pips). This gives us three chances to get our order filled, at 0.6316, at 0.6317, and also at 0.6318. We know the worst case scenario is the last of those prices, which means we would suffer a maximum slippage of 0.0002 (2 pips), and we may get in at a better price than that. Any worse than 0.6318 and the order won't execute.

Stop Order

This is the third main order type. A stop order says *"I want to buy (or sell) this pair at a certain price or worse."* Or worse? Why would we want to buy or sell at a worse price? There are a couple of reasons. One is to exit from an order that isn't working out, which we'll examine in the next section on exiting trades. The other reason would be to automatically enter a trade if the price breaks above or below a certain level. For example, if we are watching the USD/GBP pair and the price is 0.6314 and we believe it may rise, but we don't want to enter a trade until it does so, we could put in a stop order to buy at 0.6316. As long as the price remains below that, the order will not execute. As soon as the price reaches our stop price (0.6316) or passes above it, the stop order turns into a market order and executes at whatever price is available.

Because a stop order turns into a market order, it means we may get slippage when it executes. On the other hand, we can be sure that if the price reaches our stop price, we will get filled, unlike a limit order which makes no such guarantee.

Stop sell orders, of course, work just the same but in reverse. A stop sell order at 0.6314 will not execute as long as the price is above that level. As soon as the price reaches 0.6314 or falls below it, the stop sell order will become a market sell order and will execute at whatever price is available at that instant.

OCO

Sometimes we may have an idea that the price is going to move strongly, but we don't know in which direction. We want to be ready to enter a trade whether it goes up or down, because we have reason to believe that any move is going to be sustained. In such situations, a One Cancels Other, or OCO order, is the perfect tool for the job.

The OCO order is two orders in one, either a pair of stop orders or a pair of limit orders. Think of it as an upper and lower boundary on a price chart. In the case of a pair of stop orders, one part of the order will be used to buy (go long) should the price rise to a level whereby it reaches or exceeds the higher stop price. The other part of the order will sell (go short) if the price falls to meet or drop below the lower stop price. When either order triggers, the other is automatically cancelled, as we're in the trade and it's no longer required.

If the OCO is a pair of limit orders, then one part would be used to sell (go short) if the price reached or exceeded the higher limit price, and the other part would be used to buy (go long) if the price fell to or below the lower limit price. Again, as soon as one part of the order filled, the other would automatically be cancelled.

OCO orders aren't offered by all brokers. The same effect can be used even when this order isn't supported, simply send two separate stop or limit orders, and be sure to cancel one when the other is filled.

Stop Limit Order

As its name suggests, this is a hybrid stop and limit order. It works exactly the same as a stop order up until the moment the stop price is met or exceeded. At that point instead of becoming a market order, it turns into a limit order. Stop limit orders necessarily have two prices: the stop price which is the trigger to turn it into a limit order, and the limit price which specifies the minimum execution price once the order has become a limit order.

Not all brokers offer stop limit orders, but when they are available they are useful beasts indeed. As with regular limit orders they offer no guarantee of getting an order filled, but they do offer the security of knowing there will be limited (if any) slippage should the order execute successfully.

Choosing The Order Type

When entering new trades I recommend using limit and stop limit orders wherever possible. Using a limit price of the current price offset by a few pips provides you with a safety net. Should the price move quickly and violently, you will either get into a great trade at a great price, or you will miss out. Better to miss out though, than try entering with a market order and get filled some considerable distance from where you wanted to be, leaving you playing catch up right from the start.

If you use any kind of automatic order like an attached stop order, or an OCO, do keep an eye on it any make sure it executes correctly. It is not unknown for these things to suffer from gremlins every now and then. The automatic nature of these kinds of orders is to save time and clicks, not to absolve your from all responsibility of managing your account. If an automatic stop order doesn't get placed, or part of an OCO order fails to cancel itself, the broker probably won't be sympathetic. Think of these orders as being like an auto-pilot in an aircraft, you still want someone in the cockpit to keep an eye on things and make sure the systems do what they're supposed to.

Exiting Trades

When it comes to exiting trades, we need to be more flexible in the choice of order. The selection will depend on the reason we are exiting. If we're getting out because we are reaching the price target we had in mind, then a limit order is a pretty safe option. Indeed in such a situation we can enter our limit order long before the price reaches the target. We can even enter it as soon as our entry order has filled. If we put a limit order in that early, it is important to keep an eye on it throughout the duration of the trade. A price target may look reasonable at the start, but the price may not behave as we expect. It could blast through the limit price and keep going (in which case, our order will take us out too soon and we will miss out on some tasty profit), or the price may approach but just not quite make it, in which case our limit order will never execute. A limit order isn't a set-and-forget solution, it should be actively managed.

If we are exiting a trade because it hasn't worked out as we hoped, then a market order is a better option, especially if the trade is a loss. Our objective is to keep losses as small as possible. Waiting around for limit orders to get hit is not a good way of doing that. When in a losing position, we want out as fast as possible, and a market order is the best way to achieve that.

Stop Orders For Exits

Stop orders are so essential they deserve their own explanation. Remember a stop order is an order to buy or sell at a specified price or *worse*. That means a stop order as an exit order gets triggered when the price moves against us. If we are long (we bought), then a stop order to sell will be at a certain price or *lower*. If we are short (we sold), a stop order to buy will be at a certain price or *higher*. Stop orders are perfect for providing protection of our position. They can take us out of a position if the price moves a certain distance against us. They will limit our loss, or lock in at least some of our profit, depending on where they are placed. When we use stop orders in this way, we call them a *stop loss*, because they can literally stop us making a loss, or stop a loss from getting any bigger. Let's work through an example, because this is a really important order type to understand.

We will imagine we are watching the CAD/CHF (Canadian Dollar / Swiss Franc). The price of the pair is 0.9189. We decide to go long, and we buy on a limit order, getting us into the trade at the current price. We believe that the balance of probability favours the price rising (which is why we bought!), but we need to be prepared for the price falling, because we never know what is going to happen. We decide that if the price falls as far as 0.9182 then we want to get out of the trade. If the price gets that far then it will be clear to us that it is not behaving according to our analysis, the reason for our trade is no longer valid, and we want to be out without taking any greater loss than 7 pips (0.9189 − 0.9182). We enter a stop sell order with a stop price of 0.9182.

Having this order in place provides us a number of advantages. Firstly, if anything should happen to our computer or internet connection which means we no longer have access to our broker, we know that the order is there and will exit the trade for us, limiting our losses. If this order wasn't there and our internet connection went down for a couple of hours, we could conceivably log in later to find that the price had dropped massively leaving us with a huge loss.

A second advantage is that this stop order removes a decision point. If the price falls and our trade moves into loss, we know we must exit quickly keeping the loss small. However, as you will discover, *knowing* you must exit at a loss and *actually* exiting at a loss are two different things. Psychologically it can be very difficult to accept that loss, and it's all too easy to hesitate. If that happens, you can bet the price will drop even further, meaning you end up with an even bigger loss! Entering a stop order immediately after the trade has started, means that you don't have to manually place an order to exit at a loss, that order is already at the broker and will execute automatically. We will look more at the psychological aspects to trading in the Trading Mentality section.

There are two ways we can decide the stop price for our stop loss orders. The first is to use a simple offset. For example, we could say that for every trade we enter, we will set a stop loss order at 5 pips away from the entry price. If the price moves 5 pips against us, the stop gets hit and closes our trade. 5 pips is an arbitrary figure, the actual amount would depend on the type of trade we were taking. It may be that we are trading a strategy whereby if the price moves against us by just 2 pips, we know that trade hasn't worked out and we want to be out.

We always want to exit at the earliest sign things aren't working out, keeping our loss small. There's no point setting a stop too far away and then just waiting for it to get hit even though we know the trade has already failed, that would be throwing money away. On the other hand, we need to be mindful that prices rarely move smoothly, they may go up three pips, down two, up another three, down another two and so on. We need to place our stops far enough away that they let the price ebb and flow naturally, without getting hit.

The second way to decide where to put stop loss orders is to examine the chart and find a logical place. For example, if we decide to go short by buying when the price breaks down and out of a triangle, we would know that the trade had failed if the price came back up and broke above the triangle. Therefore we could place our stop order at 1 pip above the top line of the triangle. Here's how that would look on the chart:

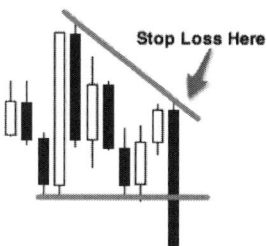

Or maybe we go long, buying as the price bounces off a support line. If the price fails to rise and instead drops below the support line then we would know that the trade had failed and we would want to be out. In that case, we would place our stop order just below the support line. Here's how that might look:

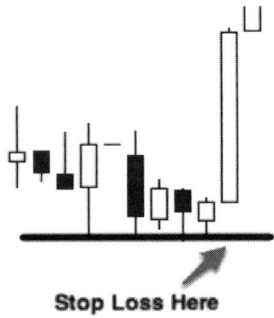

Stop Loss Here

Trailing Stops

To discover what a trailing stop is, let's go back to our earlier example. We were long CAD/CHF from 0.9189 and had a stop sell order with the broker at 0.9182. As it happens, our analysis was spot on and the price rises steadily. Within a couple of minutes it is at 0.9195. We don't want to exit yet because this is just the start of the trade and we fully expect the price to continue rising. At the same time, we know that the price could fall back, and the trade could move into a losing position. Our objective is to maximise profits and minimise losses. We can minimise our loss right here by changing our stop order. We change the stop price in the order from 0.9182 to 0.9189.

Now if the price falls away, our stop order will get hit at the same price at which we bought. If that happens, and if there is no slippage, we would exit our trade at break even. No profit, but no loss either. The trade is now effectively risk-free. We could have moved our stop price to a few pips above, say 0.9192, so that if it got hit we would at least make a couple of pips profit. However, we need to leave the price some room to move around (what I call "wiggle room"). We've seen from the price charts we've already looked at that price rarely moves continuously in one direction. If we put our stop price too close to the current price there is a risk it will get hit, taking us out of our trade, before the price continues merrily upwards without us. As we move the stop order then, we need to try and balance risk against letting the price do its thing, and staying in the trade for maximum profit.

The price continues to rise, and soon is at 0.9212. We decide to move our stop order again, this time up to 0.9200. Now if the stop order gets triggered, we will exit with 11 pips profit (assuming no slippage), and we're still leaving 12 pips wiggle room between the current price and our stop order.

As long as the price keeps going our way, we can keep moving the stop price, ratcheting it up a little at a time, locking in ever more profit. Moving a stop in this way is called *trailing*. A trailing stop is simply one that trails the current price.

Some broker platforms offer automatic trailing stops. When you place the stop order, in addition to the stop price they let you specify a trail offset—the number of pips you want the stop to follow the current price by. These automatic orders can be handy, but there are advantages to managing a trailing stop manually. Here's an example of how we might trail a stop loss order, using a mixture of a fixed offset and logical placement. The example is on the USD/CAD pair:

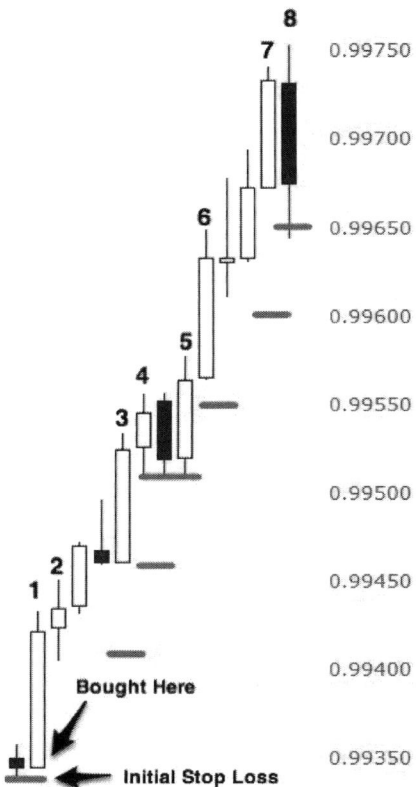

This is how this example trade was worked:

Bar 1: The start of the trade. Long USD/CAD at 0.9935. The stop loss is initially placed 1 pip below the low of the previous bar.

Bar 2: The price hits 0.9945 which means that the trade is 10 pips in profit. The stop loss is moved to 0.9936, which is break even plus one pip (to cover the spread and thus exit the trade for no loss should it turn round).

Bar 3: The price continues upwards and hits 0.9950, the trade is now 15 pips in profit. The stop loss is moved to 0.9940, keeping it at 10 pips below the price. Now if it is hit, the trade will exit with 5 pips profit.

Bar 4: The price hits 0.9955, so the trade is now 20 pips in profit. Still keeping the 10 pip offset the stop loss can be moved to 0.9945, locking in 10 pips profit if it gets hit.

Bar 5: There is very clear support below the last three bars. If the support line is broken then there's a good chance the price will continue downwards, so it makes sense to move the stop to 1 pip below this support, which is around 0.9950. Now if the it gets hit, the trade will exit with 15 pips profit.

Bar 6: The price hits 0.9965, so still keeping a 10 cent offset, the stop loss can be moved up to 0.9955, locking in 20 pips profit.

Bar 7: The price is 0.9970, so we can move the stop loss to 0.9960, locking in 25 pips profit.

Bar 8: The price reaches 0.9975, so the stop loss can be moved to 0.9965. In the same bar, the price drops, and hits the stop loss order, exiting the trade. The total profit is 30 pips (0.9965 exit price − 0.9935 entry price).

Automatic Orders

If your broker supports them, it is worth using automatic orders when you enter a new trade. We've already seen how a stop order can limit loss if a trade goes against you. These stop loss orders are so essential they should be sent the instant you enter any new position. Many brokers' order tickets will allow you to send an automatic stop order at the same time as your entry order. The stop order won't become live until your entry order has executed. If your entry order is cancelled, the associated stop order will also be cancelled.

An automatic limit order can usually be sent with an entry order as well. You would set this to your initial price target, if you have one. Again, this limit order won't become live until your entry order executes. It will also be associated with the stop order so that if the stop order executes then the limit order will be cancelled. And of course, if the limit order executes, so the stop order will be cancelled.

Scaling Out

Trailing stops are one way we can lock in profit from our trade, while still leaving it open to go on further and make even more profit. Another way is to scale out. This means instead of exiting our trade in one go, we can just exit part of our position, leaving the rest to run on and potentially make more money. Time for another example:

We are watching EUR/USD (Euro/US Dollar). The price is 1.3070. We go long, buying 100,000, which costs us $130,700 (although of course because of margin, only a fraction of that is deducted from our account—around $3000 typically).

The price rises and reaches 1.3090. This is in line with our analysis, and we had planned to exit here. However, our continuing analysis of the situation suggests that the price may continue on even higher, but we're not sure. To lock in some profit, we decide to exit half of our position. We sell 50,000 which at the current price, credits our account with $65,450. Now even if the price falls right back to where we entered and we exit the other half of our position at break even ($65,350) we will still have made $100 profit. Of course, had we exited all of our position at the higher price we would have made $200. But what if the price didn't fall back, and instead carried on right up to 1.3130? If we sold our second half there, it would be for $65,650 which combined with the sale from the previous half, would give us a total profit of $300.

Exiting half a position means we get to say *"I'm taking some of this profit right now, no matter what happens next"*. In times of uncertainty, it gives us the possibility to stay partially in the trade at no risk; we've already made some profit and it's safely in our account. From a psychological point of view, scaling out of a position like this takes an enormous weight off the shoulders. It's a great way to stay in a trade and let it run on to its full potential.

Money Management

Our objective is to win more trades than we lose, and win bigger than we lose. Regardless of how well we meet this objective, one thing is certain: losing trades will happen. Indeed they will happen with a regularity that to the novice trader can appear quite alarming. They are nothing to worry about, they are part of the job of trading. The only way to avoid losing trades altogether is to not trade at all. As we know these losses are going to come along, we need to make sure we plan for them and trade accordingly. That means not risking too much of our account on any single trade. We must manage our money in a way that gives us the best chance of staying solvent. We don't want to get hit with a couple of massive losses that clean us out.

This money management is very simple. We need to devise a strategy for how much of our account we can safely risk on any given trade, assuming that we will at some point get hit by a string of losing trades. Every trader's money management plan will be unique to them, and will depend on their own trading style, frequency, their account size, and to a certain degree their experience (all traders expect losing trades, no matter how experienced they are). For example, let's imagine we have a trading account with $2,000 in. Our broker requires that we maintain a minimum balance of $1,000. We plan to take profits out of our account every time it reaches a balance of $3,000. We'll take out a thousand out each time, bringing us back to our $2,000 balance. We take an average of two trades each day. We want to plan for a worst case scenario, which could be for example, that we lose every trade we take for a week straight. That would be ten trades in all (2 trades per day x 5 trading days in the week). The most money we can lose is $1,000 because after that our account balance will be too low and the broker may close our account. So in this scenario, we could risk $100 per trade. If we lost every trade for a week, and each trade lost the maximum we were prepared to risk, we would lose our $1,000 (10 trades x $100 risked on each trade).

Knowing that we can afford to lose a maximum of $100 per trade means we can now weigh up the risk of each trade that comes our way. If we see a potential trade setting up, we would look at where we expect to exit if that trade failed, which is to say where we would be placing our stop loss order. If that exit point would mean potentially losing more than $100 on the trade, we would not enter. The risk of loss would exceed the maximum allowed by our money management strategy.

Knowing up front the maximum amount we can lose in any given day takes off a lot of the psychological pressure that we can feel when trading. Starting the day with the assumption that we will lose every trade might sound a little pessimistic, but it's not a bad mindset to have. Too many traders think about how much money they can make from each trade, and not enough about how much they might lose. Realistically not every trade will be a winner, not even close. A clear money management methodology such as that presented here, is essential to long term success in trading.

Chapter Five

Trading Strategy

Throughout this book I have alluded to having a trading strategy, a means by which we can choose when and where to enter and exit trades. Now is the time to look at how we can create such a strategy. It may seem quite late to have got to this point, but everything discussed so far forms part of the groundwork for our strategy. There is little point in nailing down chart patterns before we understand what makes those patterns appear. No use either in working out where we'll place stop loss orders if we don't appreciate what they are and why they are so essential. Now that we have these foundations in place, we can build our castle. Our trading strategy is simply our set of guidelines for when and what to buy and sell. I say guidelines and not rules, because we need to maintain a degree of flexibility in our trading, otherwise we may as well have a computer trade for us.

A Word on Automation

Computer trading is not uncommon. The only people doing it really successfully are the big players—the banks and institutions. They can employ very powerful equipment programmed with extremely complex algorithms designed by the best in the business, to chip away taking tiny profits but in huge quantities. This kind of program trading is only viable with the exceptionally low commissions these guys are dealing with. Program trading isn't limited to micro-trades, there are longer term algorithms at work too.

Down at our end of the scale there are no shortage of trading programs, or robots, available off the shelf. Some are profitable for a time. Few are profitable over the long term. None are as profitable as a skilled human trader. Programs follow rules, *we* can bend them. We have the advantage of being able to look at a chart and say *"This pattern meets all the criteria for our rule that says 'buy here', but I can see something on this chart which means the trade is never going to work out!"* Rules, by their very nature, have to deal in generalities. We cannot have a rule for every single possible permutation of a chart. We can start off simply, by looking for a trend and trying to follow it. Then we have to add in some filters to say don't follow it if this or that happens. If we add too many filters, our rule will never be triggered. Not enough and we may find we enter too many losing trades. Rules are inflexible.

Human traders on the other hand, are infinitely flexible. We can see a chart that meets all the criteria for a rule and say *"I've seen a chart just like this a few times and it never works out."* We can learn from history. We can spot subtle nuances. We can see obvious opportunities for a great trade where no rule exists to say *"Take this great trade."* The downside to this flexibility is that we have to be able to execute on our thoughts. We must have the courage of our convictions when it comes to clicking the buy or sell button. It sounds easy in theory, but when we have money in the market and stand to lose it, our minds can play tricks on us and try to stop us carrying out our strategy. We need to be able to think like a person and act like a machine, it's not always easy.

Ultimately what we are trying to do is figure out whether the majority of participants (people) think the price will rise or fall. We are trading the views of other people, we need to think like those people. That's something we can do, and computers cannot (yet!)

The Purpose Of This Section

In this section my aim is to give you a framework strategy, something you can start using right away. However, every trader can and should develop their strategy over time, making it truly their own. As you grow as a trader, you will discover areas in which you are stronger, and you should play to these. It may well be that you start out with the intention of being a pure day trader, but that over time you find you are better at picking out longer term trends and swing trading them over days or even weeks. At the other end of the spectrum, you might find that you don't have the patience for any trade that lasts longer than twenty minutes. Time frames are just one aspect of trading. Other personality traits and sensibilities will include your ability to keep track of multiple charts, or just a couple. Some traders excel at being a specialist in just one or two currency pairs. They get to know those pairs inside out, becoming very much part of the club. Remember we are trading with real people, and the more time we spend with those people the better we will be at reading their actions and reactions. Specialising in one or two pairs gives a trader the chance to learn every nuance of how those pairs move. Over time they can see all sorts of different trade opportunities on a single chart, and almost always be in a trade one way or the other.

Yet other traders will find that their skill set lies in rapidly scanning through many currency pairs, looking for just one or two very specific chart patterns that they know inside out. They don't have preferred pairs, but preferred trade setups.

The fact is that traders are as unique and individual as any other people. It is not my place to tell you how you should trade, but to show you a variety of setups to get you going, a starter pack if you like. These will get you on the road, they will start you on your journey. As you progress it is your job to find out what kind of trader you are, and to adapt your plan accordingly. You may throw out some or all of these setups, replacing them with your own. Or you may add to them. The choice is yours.

MISSION: As you progress through this section, learning each new setup, start looking for that setup when you practice looking at charts each day. Try and spot the setup patterns, and then look at how you would have traded them according to what you've learnt.

Types of Trade Setup

Our framework strategy is a collection of trade setups. When choosing trade setups there are three main ways we can go: trend following, trend change, and event driven.

Trend following setups are those where we trade in the same direction as the trend. In this case we are talking about the immediate term trend rather than any longer term trend. These kinds of setup are the least risky because when the price is heading in a particular direction, it takes more energy for it to change direction than to continue. The path of least resistance is to keep going the same way. Thus there is a higher probability that the price will continue or go sideways, than change direction completely. That means any trend following setup starts out with a good dose of probability on our side. All we can ever do is weigh up these probabilities and try and put as much in our favour as possible, so starting out with any probability on our side is very much a good thing.

Trend change setups are quite the opposite. Such trades seek to find the top or bottom of the current short term trend, then jump into a trade as the price turns around and starts a new trend. This is a much riskier way to trade because spotting a change in trend is more difficult than recognising the fact that the price is already in a trend. The payoff though, is that if we are able to get in at the start of a trend we can capture much more of that trend, meaning bigger profits on winning trades.

The final major category of setup is the event driven trade. These are not looking to get in on any trend, rather they seek to take advantage of specific events that can drive the price quickly in any direction.

Because we want to be able to trade whatever the prevailing market conditions are, we will use setups that fall into each of these categories in our framework strategy.

Setup Number 1: Inside Bar

This first setup is trend following. We are looking to take a chunk of profit from an established trend. It is very low risk, and the setup itself provides us with a very clear entry signal and a clear exit should the trade fail. Firstly, let's look at the entry signal, a bar pattern called the inside bar. We are looking for two consecutive bars that make the following pattern:

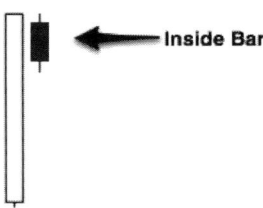

At its most basic level, the inside bar pattern comprises two bars, with the range of the second bar being contained entirely within the range of the first bar. This shows consolidation in place. If we were to zoom in and display the same two bars on a smaller timescale, we would see a triangle pattern. Taken by this simple criteria alone, an inside bar pattern is very common, and we certainly don't want to trade every single one that comes along. We need to add some more filters to pick out just the best patterns, those which have a good chance of following through with predictable movement. Because we are seeing consolidation, the follow through we are looking for would be a continuation of a trend before the price paused and consolidated. For any continuation of a trend, there needs to be a trend to continue! So our first filter will be that the pattern must occur within a trend, either up or down. That means we need to look at the bars that come before the two which form the pattern itself:

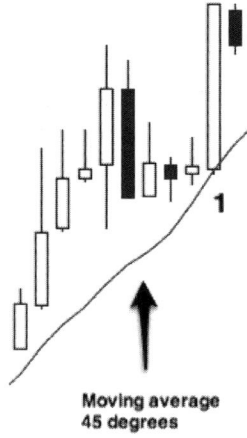

Moving average
45 degrees

How many bars back we look is something we can experiment with. Look too far back and we risk getting in right at the end of a trend when there's nothing left for us to grab. If we don't look back far enough, we risk seeing a trend where in reality there is none. I would suggest starting with 10 bars as a good compromise. As well as looking just at the price bars, we can use a moving average indicator to show us if there is a trend. In the chart segment above I have added a 10 period SMA. We can see that it is angled at approximately 45 degrees by the time the inside bar pair of bars comes along. Such an angle is a good indication that we are in an up trend. The fact that the first bar of our inside bar pair bounces off the MA (shown as point 1 on the chart) is a bonus signal that the price is on the rise—the MA has provided *support*.

Another filter we can use is the size and position of the second bar in relation to the first. In this example, the second bar is much smaller than the first one, showing a tight consolidation. It is also positioned right at the top of the first bar. When consolidation happens at one extreme of the previous bar like this, it is a sign that the price is set to move further in that direction. Of course, if the second bar was at the bottom of the range set by the preceding bar, that would not be a good sign at all. Indeed looking at the middle of our example chart we can see that there is another inside bar pattern (shown below as number 1), with the second bar positioned at the bottom of the previous bar. We would not want to trade this because the consolidation is not in the same direction as the trend. The second pattern (2) in in line with the trend and so is one we would be interested in trading.

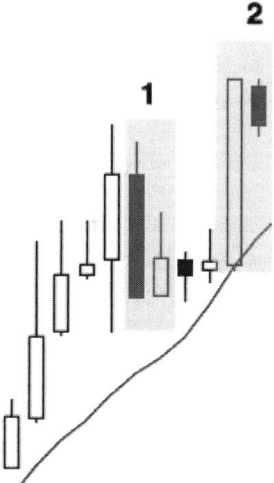

To summarise then, we could define our inside bar setup signal as follows:

1. An inside bar pattern must occur within an existing trend.

2. The existing trend is defined by a 10 period moving average, which must be angled and not flat.

3. The second bar of the inside bar pattern must be smaller than the first bar, and must occur at the top of the first bar in an up trend or the bottom of the first bar in a down trend.

If we find a pattern that meets all these criteria, then we would look to enter our trade when the price exceeds the high or low set by the first bar in the inside bar pair (bar 1 below). In this example, as we are looking at an up trend, we would *buy* when the price exceeded the high of that bar. If we were watching a down trend, we would *sell* when the price dropped below the low. Here's the chart again showing where the price must cross to signal an entry:

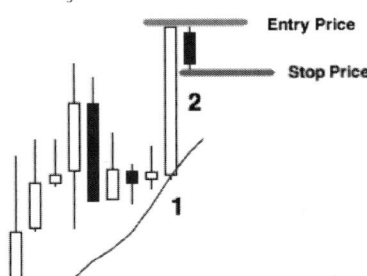

The pattern also gives us a convenient place to locate our stop loss order. If the price falls below the low of the second bar in the pattern (bar 2 above), we will consider the trade to have failed and will exit.

We have another opportunity here to add a filter to our trade setup. We could decide that we will only trade if the bar immediately following the pattern, crosses the entry price. If we wanted to be more lenient, we could trade on *any* subsequent break above the entry price, whether that happened on the next bar or five bars later. Or we could compromise and say that we will enter on the next two bars, three bars, or whatever we decide is reasonable. The longer we wait for a break of the entry price to happen, the less chance it has of being successful. That's because what we are hoping for is pent-up energy to be released after the consolidation which occurs in the second bar of the inside bar pattern. If the break happens quickly, that energy will be released in a flurry of trading, carrying the price with it. If it takes ages for the break to happen, then most of that energy will already have dispersed.

The decision on how long to wait for a break is a great example of how human traders have a big advantage over automated systems. An automatic trading program will always follow the same rule. We can have a guideline that simply says *"Enter on a break above or below the inside bar pattern"*, and we can use our judgement as to whether or not the pattern is still valid. We can look at the next few bars, and interpret what is happening. If they stay tight, keeping in the same sort of range, then we know that the consolidation is ongoing. If the price moves all over the place, then we can see that the consolidation is over and there is no consensus on direction. We want to always be *reading* the chart, interpreting what we see, and allowing it to shape our trading decisions.

Back to our example chart, and here's what happened with this particular pattern:

In fact the bar immediately after the inside bar pattern (bar 1 above) did not break above the entry price. But it did remain in the same tight range. The next bar (bar 2) broke above, and so we could have bought (gone long) as it crossed above the line. As we can see from the chart, the price rose steadily for two consecutive bars, before switching to sideways movement.

That got us into the trade, what about deciding when to exit? We already know where we would exit if the price was to fall—as soon as it crossed the low of the second bar in the inside bar pattern (the lower horizontal line on the above chart). In this case though, the trade was profitable. We could have moved our stop loss order to break even as soon as the trade was profitable, and as the price continued to rise, we could have moved it again to lock in some profit should the price have suddenly turned round and dropped back down. Indeed, trailing our stop in this way is one possible exit strategy. We could simply have chosen to keep ratcheting up our stop until eventually it got hit.

If we don't want to use a trailing stop, then we can use the chart to tell us where to exit. I've marked some possible exits on this chart:

Bar 3: When there are three subsequent bars that go against the direction of the trade. As this trade was a long, we could exit when we saw three consecutive bars make lower prices.

Bar 4. As soon as the price crossed the moving average. We used the moving average to determine that we were in an up trend, so the price crossing below it is a good signal that the trend has come to an end.

Bar 4. Less conservatively, we could wait for a price bar to *close* below the moving average. Often the price will dip below an MA only to go back in its original direction. Waiting for a price bar to close below it is a stronger signal that the price is changing direction. In this particular example, the first bar to cross the MA also closed below it, so the signal was the same. But that's not always the case.

Not marked on this chart, but equally valid, we could exit once we saw the moving average line go flat. That's somewhat more subjective than a hard and fast rule like the three above, but again we're humans not machines and we're pretty good at judging subjective criteria like this.

Here's another example, this time trading short:

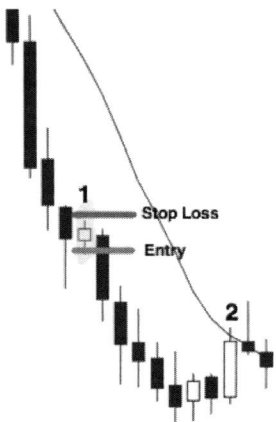

The price is in a down trend, the steep angle of the Moving Average makes that very clear. The highlighted bar 1 is the inside bar. It's not as near to the extremity of the previous bar as the earlier example, making this a riskier trade. Because the price is dropping, we are looking to sell short, our entry being on a break below the low of the inside bar. Our stop loss order can be placed above the high of that same bar. As we can see from the chart segment, the price dropped on the very next bar, so we would have sold short. Our account would be credited with the proceeds of the sale.

To exit, we could either have trailed our stop loss order, or waited for the price to break above the moving average, which happened on the bar labelled 2. We would exit the trade by buying back the same quantity we had sold. Because the price was lower, this purchase would cost us less than we were credited from the short sale, the difference is our profit.

Of course, patterns and setups like this only give us clues about what may happen next. They show us where the balance of probability lies, but they are not perfect, and no pattern works every time.

Here's an example of an inside bar setup that failed, making a loss rather than a profit:

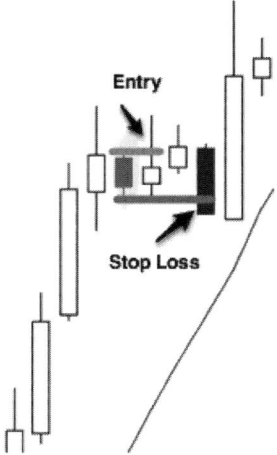

Once again the price is in a strong upwards trend, as confirmed by the steep angle of the moving average. The pattern has formed, the inside bar is around the middle of the previous bar, so again this is a sign to be cautious. The pattern isn't perfect, but neither is it obviously bad. Because we are in an up trend we are looking to buy if the price breaks above the high of the inside bar. It does so on the next bar. Our stop loss order is placed just below the low of the inside bar. Although the price starts to rise, it does so somewhat halfheartedly, and then falls sharply, at which point it hits the stop loss order which exits us from the trade. The loss is only small, which is the most important thing. If we were trailing the stop loss order behind the price, ratcheting it up once the trade moved into profit, then the loss may have been even smaller. However, in this case the price was in profit only for a very short time and by a small amount, so there wasn't really a good opportunity to move the stop loss before it was hit.

As it happens, after this trade was stopped out, the price rose again. When this happens it can be tempting to jump back in, opening another trade quickly, trying to recoup the loss. Unless there is a valid setup to warrant doing so, this is not the right thing to do! The setup has been and gone, and in this case it did not work out. Our job is not to chase the price, it is just to trade the setups as they come along. Although the trade was a loss, provided we entered and exited where we were supposed to, we can count the trade as a success and move on to look for the next one.

Make It Your Own

In this setup I've given you some guidelines for determining if there is a trade to take, as well as some suggestions for how to exit the trade. If you choose to use this pattern, you can make it your own by testing and tweaking the following parameters:

Confirmation of trend. You can use a certain number of bars, or look for a trend line, or use a moving average. If you use an MA, you can tweak the number of periods used. Longer periods will require stronger trends to show a good angle, but those trends will be less frequent.

Exit signal. Using more lax exit signals, like waiting for the price to close below a moving average, will keep you in trades for longer. But that can come at the expense of giving back some of the profit the trade has made. Conservative signals will get you out more quickly, but you may miss out on secondary and even tertiary moves giving more profit.

Break above / below the entry price. The inside bar pattern sets the price at which you enter, but you have some leeway in deciding whether or not the break of that price must occur immediately following the pattern.

Setup Number 2: Pin Bar

This is another bar / candlestick pattern. We use it to spot a change in the immediate direction of price. Here's what the pattern looks like, as candlesticks and as bars:

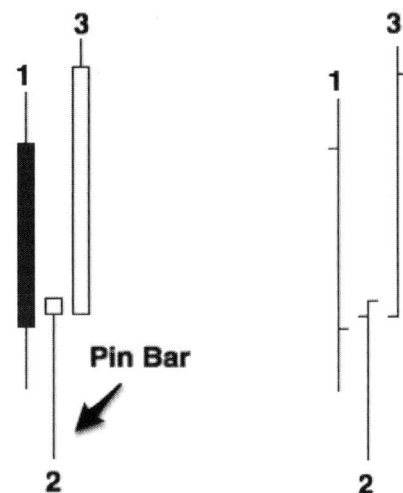

These are the important characteristics we are looking for:

- The *pin bar* itself is the middle bar in a three bar formation (bar number 2 above). Its most obvious attribute is its very long wick (most evident when viewed as a candlestick).

- The open and close prices of the pin bar should fall within the range of the bars on either side (bars 1 and 3). Note that they don't need to fall within the open and close price of those surrounding bars, just within the range as a whole.

- The open and close prices of the pin bar should be close together. The closer they are, the stronger the signal (we'll see why in a second).

- The open and close prices of the pin bar should be towards the end of the bar.

What's so special about this pattern? If we think about what these three bars are showing us, it becomes quite clear. We can see from bar 1 that the price is dropping. The bar is a good size and there is some distance between the open and the close, the price fell a long way. The story changes in bar 2. Although the price again fell a long way down, it managed to regain all of that fall, and even rose a little. In other words, the consensus view of price direction changed fundamentally, so much so that enough people switched from selling to buying to reverse the whole of the fall seen in bar 2, and still keep going. Bar 3 confirms this change in price direction by pushing on upwards. The majority view at this point seems to be very clearly that the price is going up!

There are two possible entry points we can trade with this setup:

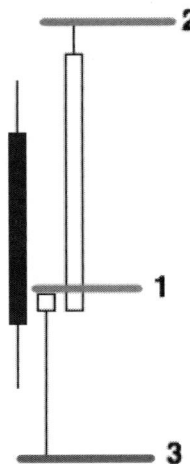

Option 1: The most aggressive entry is as soon as the price breaks above the high of the pin bar itself (line 1 above). In this case we are trading the instant the pattern becomes fully formed. We need to take care that the low of the third bar encompasses the open and close of the pin bar, in order that the pin bar itself is valid. Using this entry is more risky as we don't see confirmation of the price direction from the third bar, so we may see fewer winners. The reward for that risk is that when the trade works out, we capture more of the move and therefore more profit. It also means we risk losing much less if the trade fails, because our entry will be closer to our stop loss.

Option 2: If we want to be more conservative we can wait for the third bar to complete fully, confirming the change of direction in the price, and then enter when the price breaks above the high of that bar (line 2 above).

Our stop loss order can be placed just below the low of the bar immediately before the pin bar (line 3 on the chart). If the price drops below that point then the pattern has failed and we need to be out of the trade.

Although we will see more failed trades by entering using option 1, the much lower loss from having the stop loss so much nearer the entry price, and the greater profit from capturing more of the move, outweigh the few extra losing trades. Because of that I recommend using option 1 as the entry.

Here's how this example trade worked out:

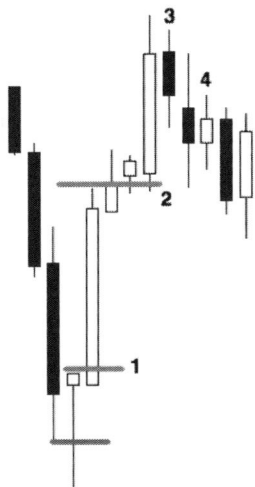

I've included the preceding bars here to give a little more context to the setup. As we can see, the price was falling fast, with three good down bars before the pin bar. An entry taken at point 1 or 2 would both have yielded a profit.

To exit, we have a few options again. Firstly of course, we have our stop loss. We would have entered a stop at the red line as soon as our entry order was filled, to keep us out of trouble if we lost our connection to the broker. Once the trade was in profit, we could then move the stop order up, locking in some of those gains. As with the previous setup, we could continue to trail our stop order, and let that exit us from the trade when it eventually got hit.

Another possible exit was the bar at point 3. This bar retraced a large part of the previous bar's gains, so it is a signal that this move upwards may be over, at least for now. A more conservative exit would be to wait for three bars against us, which would take us out at point 4. In this example, that would have cost us some of our profit, but in another trade it may have let the price run on further, making more pips. Once again, as human traders we aren't bound by hard and fast rules. We can continually read the chart, try and interpret the sentiment, and adapt accordingly. The two down bars between point 3 and point 4 are a strong retracement. Prior to those bars we saw three strong down bars, the pin bar, then four consecutive up bars. These are five minute bars, so we know that the price dropped cleanly for fifteen minutes, switched direction at the pin bar, then rose cleanly for twenty minutes. Based on that prior action, ten minutes of falling price would be enough to suggest that the move is over and it is time to get out.

It's important to understand that we're not making decisions based on our own emotions here. We don't want to exit because we're afraid to lose the profit we've made.

We must trade based on what the chart tells us.

Here's an example of a pin bar signalling the continuation of a down trend:

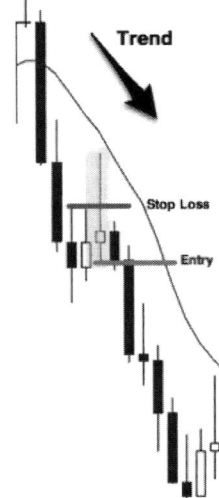

We can see from the moving average that the trend is clearly downwards. The price retraces for a couple of bars, the second of which becomes a pin bar (highlighted). The pin bar carries some additional strength from the fact that it bounces just short of the moving average, giving us a confluence of signals that the price is set to drop. The aggressive entry option is to sell short when the price breaks the low of the pin bar. The stop loss order can be placed just above the high of the bar immediately preceding the pin bar, which also happens to be an area of resistance making it a great place for a stop order. As we can see, the price fell away nicely, making this a profitable trade. To exit we could use a trailing stop, or maybe stay in and wait until the price breaks through the moving average, depending on how aggressive we want to be.

Not every pin bar setup works out, here's an example where things didn't go according to plan:

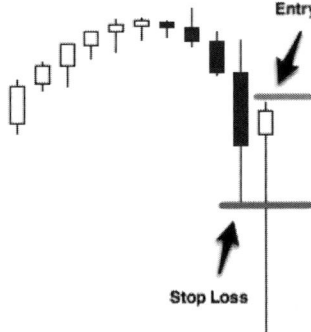

Here the price has been rising, before falling back a for a few bars. A potential pin bar has formed, which if confirmed, would suggest the price is going to start going back up. We need the next bar to engulf the range between the open and close prices of this pin bar in order to confirm it really is a pin bar. If that happens, we can buy to go long if the price breaks above the high of the pin bar, setting our stop loss sell order just below the low of the previous bar. Here's what happened next:

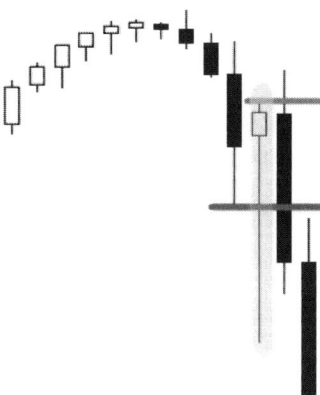

The next bar did engulf the pin bar's open and close prices, confirming the pin bar pattern. The price also rose above the high of the pin bar, so we would have bought to open our trade. However, instead of continuing its upward journey, we can see that the price fell heavily, easily falling below our stop loss order. So our stop would have sold, taking us out of the trade for a small loss.

Whilst this is a valid setup and a valid example of a failed trade, it's not a perfect pin bar setup. The price rise prior to the pin bar was already running out of steam as we can see from the ever shorter bars. Also, the pin bar itself has a relatively large range between the open and close (a large candlestick body). These two factors would give the more experienced trader pause for thought before taking the trade.

Make It Your Own

The pin bar is a nice easy to spot pattern, and it has a high success rate. The pattern is well defined, but you have some leeway in how you trade it. Here are a few ways you can make it your own:

Bigger picture. Look at the bigger trend, and only take trades in the direction of that trend.

More signals. Combine the pin bar pattern with a second signal such as a bounce off support or resistance, or off a moving average.

Go sideways. The pattern can appear in a sideways market as well as a trending one, here's an example:

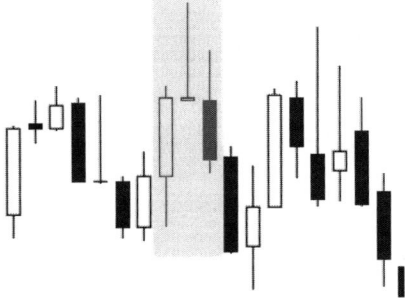

Here there is no overall direction, the price is just oscillating within a range. Even so, there is a perfect pin bar pattern. Traded with a tight trailing stop this can be a quick and profitable little trade.

Setup Number 3: Engulfing Candlestick

A candlestick can be said to *engulf* the previous candlestick if its body is wider than the body of the previous candle. Here are some examples:

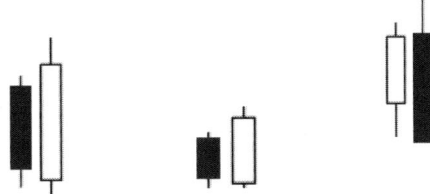

In each case, the body of the second candle literally engulfs the first. The signal is clear: whatever was going on in the first candle has come to an end, things have changed, and the price is going the other way, decisively. Although this pattern can be used to signal a change in trend, it has a much higher success rate when traded with the trend. Let's look at that last example in the context of the bars that preceded it.

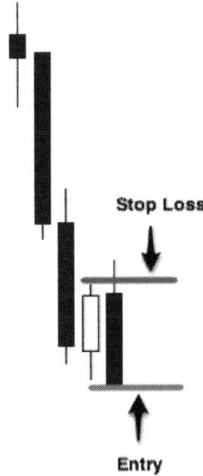

The price had been falling, before a temporary reprise. The single white bar is what we call a *pullback*, the price literally pulls back up and regains some of the loss. The bar immediately after the white pullback then engulfs it. This tells us that whatever buying was going on in that white bar, has been overwhelmed by selling. The price has lost all of the gains it made in the pullback and more besides. The suggestion here is clearly that the price is set to continue its fall. The entry is very simple, we would sell short as soon as the price drops below the low of the engulfing bar. Our stop loss can be placed just above the high of the bar preceding it.

Here's how this particular pattern worked out:

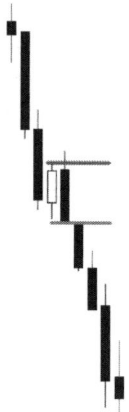

The next bar triggered our entry immediately, as the price fell below the low of the engulfing bar. It carried on down providing us with a tidy profit. To exit profitable trades, we can use all the same guidelines as the previous two setups: trailing stops, breaks of a moving average, three bars against us, or a clear signal from the price itself that the move is over.

Here's another example of the pattern in action:

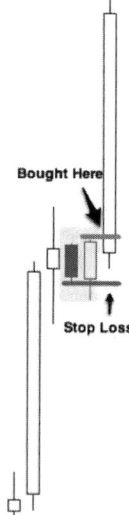

The engulfing pattern is highlighted. This time the price was rising. It fell back a little, then the engulfing bar signalled the price was set to rise further. When the bar completed we could have placed a stop buy order 1 pip above the high of the engulfing bar. When this was hit it would have taken us into a long trade. Our stop loss order could then be placed 1 pip below the low of the bar immediately preceding the engulfing bar. In this trade the stop loss wasn't hit, the trade was a very profitable winner as we can see by the strong price rise in the next bar. Not every trade works out though, as this next example shows:

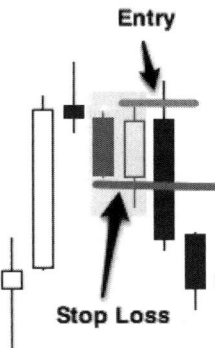

In this chart segment we see the price rising, then falling back for two bars. Next, an engulfing white candle forms, suggesting the rise is set to continue again. A stop buy order is placed 1 pip above the high of the engulfing bar. That gets hit, taking us long. We immediately enter our stop loss (sell) order 1 pip below the bar prior to the engulfing bar. We don't have to wait long to see the price turn back down and hit that stop order, closing out the trade for a loss. This trade failed, but the loss was small, far smaller than the win from the previous trade. Keeping these losses small means we are profitable overall.

Make It Your Own

This is a very simple pattern with little room for interpretation. In my definition, for a candlestick to count as engulfing, every data point should exceed the previous candle. So for example, for a white candle engulfing a black candle, the open should be lower than the previous candle's close, the close should be higher than the previous candle's open, the high should be higher than the previous high, and the low should be lower than the previous low, like this:

However, some people are happy to accept candles as engulfing where only body of the candle engulfs the body of the previous candle. They do not worry about the wick (the high and low) engulfing the previous candles wick. So this *could* be deemed an engulfing candle:

The success rate of this variety of the pattern is a little lower. I would suggest if you want to use this version of the pattern, that you do so only in conjunction with another signal which provides confirmation.

You may wish to use the engulfing pattern to try and spot the start of a new trend, and it's certainly capable of indicating such an event. The rate of success will be lower, but the profits when it does work out can be much greater. Even so, for the novice trader I recommend sticking to using the pattern in the direction of the trend.

As always there is scope for managing the exit on profitable trades using this pattern. My own preference is for a fairly tight trailing stop, but you can use your preferred signal such as a break of the moving average.

Setup Number 4: Simple News Trade

We saw earlier in the book how certain news events can have a powerful effect on currency prices. Looked at from the scale of a daily chart (each bar representing 24 hours), these events blend into the action. We may see longer bars on days where major news comes out, but nothing out of the ordinary. Zoom in to an intraday chart where each bar represents minutes, and the effect is quite different. The news event becomes obvious. Here's a chart segment for GBP/USD covering a morning when a regular weekly news release took place. Can you spot when that might have happened?

Pretty clear right? The move that starts at 8:30EST is when the US Weekly Jobless Claims figure was announced. It covers a total of 58 pips. Big and sudden moves like this clearly offer us an opportunity to make quick and generous profits. Get on the wrong side though, and we'll be looking at equally quick and large losses. We need a setup that can mitigate that risk, and give us a good chance of capturing some of the profit. *Some* is the key word here.

Trying to get all of the profit out of any move is hard. To try is to essentially guess when a move is starting and which direction it is going in. We don't want to guess, we want to have a better than 50% chance of being right. We need to be on the side of probability, and to do that we need some sign that a move has started and where it's going. Waiting for a move to start may mean we miss out on some of the profit on offer, but it means we will have a higher rate of success, more winning trades than losing ones.

How can we capture some of a move like this? The simple news trade is a very basic setup that has relatively low risk. We will use a 15 minute chart. We know when news releases with potential to move the price are scheduled to happen, and we can also deduce which currency pairs they are likely to affect. In this example, the news was US Jobless Claims, released at 08:30EST. These unemployment stats are for the US, so clearly are most likely to impact on USD pairs. The high volume pairs here are the majors like GBP/USD, EUR/USD, and so on. When you have some experience in trading this setup you can trade it on multiple pairs at the same time. Here though we'll concentrate just on this GBP/USD pair.

To trade this setup, we wait for the news release to happen. Most major figures like these are released on the hour or half past the hour, with a few coming at a quarter to or a quarter past. Whatever the case, they always happen at the start of one of our 15 minute bars. We wait for that 15 minute bar to complete. In this example, this is how that looks:

08:30 News Bar

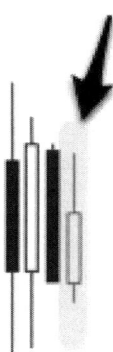

The highlighted bar starts at 08:30EST, the time of the news release, and ends at 08:45EST. This bar encompasses the frantic directionless trading that often occurs immediately following the news release. As traders hear the figures for the first time, their reactions will be mixed, causing the price to shoot up and down wildly. As the numbers are analysed, a consensus view begins to emerge, and a direction begins to set in. By the time this fifteen minute period is over, there is a high probability the direction has been set for the next few bars.

So our trade is very simply this: at the start of the next bar after the news bar completes, we buy (go long) if the news bar closed up, or we sell (go short) if the news bar closed down. In this example, the news bar closed up (which we see as a white candlestick), so we would buy as soon as the next bar starts. Our stop loss order is placed just below the low price of the news bar.

Here's how that looks in our example:

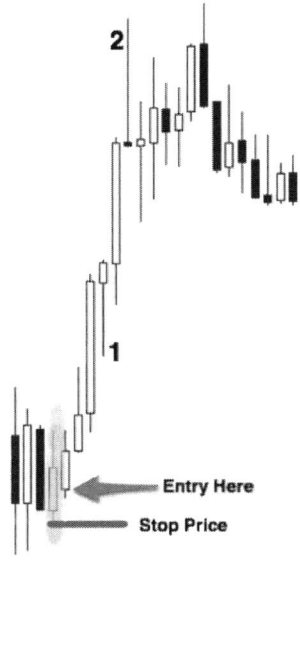

Entry Here

Stop Price

8 a   9 a   10 a   11 a   12 p   1 p :

The news bar (highlighted) closed up. We buy the instant the next bar opens. As soon as our buy order is filled we enter our stop loss order just below the low price of the news bar. If the trade failed, our stop order would exit for us.

In this case the trade worked out. The next question is where to exit? Of course, we can as with the other setups, trail our stop loss order, locking in progressively more profit as the price rises. If we chose to do this, there is a good chance our stop would have been hit on the bar labelled number 1 above, as the price dropped back considerably before continuing its ascent.

We could alternatively choose to be more aggressive in our trade, keep the stop order further back allowing more wiggle room, and letting the chart give us a clear signal as to when the move was over. The bar labelled number 2 is a very clear sign that the move up is over, at least for now. The price rose and then retraced almost all of that movement, all within the same 15 minute period. Indeed, you may recognise that as a pin bar! We know a pin bar often precedes a change in direction, so here the chart was giving us a clear signal to exit. We could even have sold short on the bar following the pin bar. With a tight stop it may have made a few pips extra profit, but the chances are that second trade would have stopped us out at or around break even.

Back on our original news trade, and I just wanted to point out that I did not include a moving average on this chart. That's because a moving average by its very nature, lags the price somewhat. By the time it caught up with the sudden movement made by the news bar, the trade was probably over. When trading news like this, moving averages don't offer us much at all.

Of course, news bar setups like all other setups, work equally well to the short side. Here's another example:

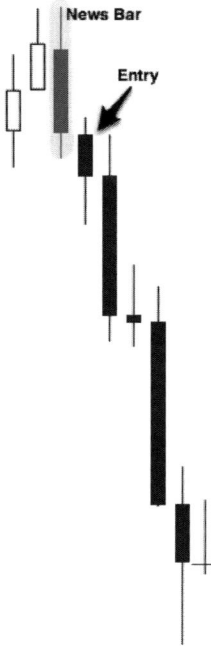

Here the news bar closed down, so we would have sold short immediately at the start of the next bar, The price fell away sharply, this would have been a very profitable trade. Not all trades are profitable, here's an example of a failed news trade:

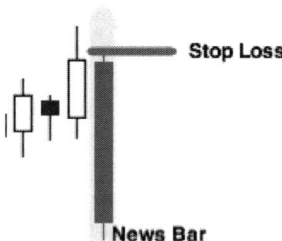

Here's a news bar that closed down. We are therefore going to go short by selling as soon as the next bar starts. Our stop loss order is placed just above the high of the news bar. Here's what happened next:

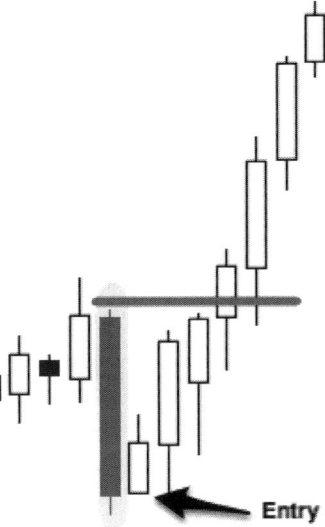

Having sold short, the price shot skywards! Our stop loss was hit, exiting the trade with a fair size loss, and the price just carried on going. This example shows that the large size of a news bar obliges us to place our stop loss order quite some way from our entry, so any loss is relatively large. We could use a tighter fixed offset stop loss, but there is another way to avoid bad trades like this one, as we will see in the next setup.

Make It Your Own

This is a very simple setup, but there are still some parameters you can tweak. The first and most obvious is the chart period. Fifteen minutes works well because it gives a reasonable amount of time for the news to sink in and a consensus view to emerge, but it is by no means set in stone. Using a longer period will give more time for a direction to emerge, which should mean fewer losing trades. That comes at the expense of smaller profits from the winners, as entries will occur later in the move when more of the rise or fall has already happened. A shorter period bar will have the opposite effect, more losers but a bigger slice of the pie on the ones that do work out. You can adapt according to what suits you better.

Exits, as always, provide plenty of scope for tailoring this setup to your own trading personality. If you prefer set-and-forge" type trades, then an automatic trailing stop loss is a no-brainer. If you are more hands on and prefer to squeeze out every last pip available, then reading the chart bar by bar is the way to go.

Finally, the position of the stop loss as we have just seen, can lead to larger losses than are ideal. An alternative position such as mid-way between the high and low of the news bar could be used, or even a straightforward fixed position stop of 5 pips away from the entry price. When altering the stop loss position, always remember that the tighter the stop, the higher the risk of it getting hit. We should always allow some room for the price to wiggle.

Setup Number 5: News Straddle

A variation of the simple news trade is the news straddle. In this version, rather than waiting for consensus on direction to be reached and then trading in the direction of the news bar, we put orders in on each side of the news bar and let the market decide which gets hit. Here's an example which shows how simple this can be:

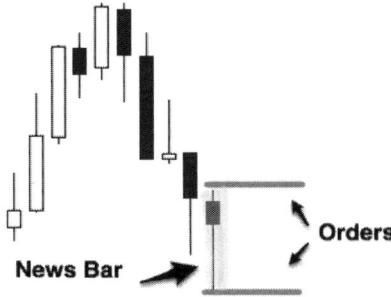

The news bar is highlighted. As soon as it completes, instead of entering a trade in the direction it closed in, we place two orders into the market. One is a stop buy order, placed 1 pip above the high of the news bar. The other is a stop sell order 1 pip below the low of the news bar. These orders *straddle* the news bar, hence the name of this setup.

If the price rises, the stop buy order will trigger and we will be in a long trade. If the price drops, the stop sell will trigger and we will find ourselves in a short trade. If the stop buy triggers, we would leave the stop sell order in place as our stop loss order. Similarly, if the stop sell order fills, we would leave the stop buy order open as our stop loss, to take us out of our short position if the trade went bad.

The advantage of using a pair of orders instead of blindly buying or selling in the same direction as the news bar is that we can enter our trade earlier, we don't need to wait for the direction to be clearly established on the chart. The bars on this chart segment are only 5 minutes each. By entering our straddle order pair we are getting into a trade 10 minutes earlier than we would with the simple news trade. There is a higher chance of the trade being a loser for the reasons mentioned in the prior setup, but if that happens we'll make a smaller loss because the range of the shorter period (5 minute) news bar is generally smaller than the 15 minute bar, and our stop loss position is dictated by that range.

Of course, we could use a 5 minute bar like this and enter a sell order as per the simple news trade (because the news bar direction was down). However, by using the dual stop orders, we're giving the market a bit more time to decide on its direction. The price still has to rise or fall a bit for one of our orders to trigger. In other words, this setup lets us enter the trade earlier than the simple news trade, but it still gives the market time and space to show us the direction the price wants to move in. It's a pretty good compromise all round. Let's see how the trade worked out in this example:

In this case, the price rose substantially and quickly. The stop buy order would have triggered, and we would have left the stop sell in place as our stop loss order.

If we had used these 5 minute bars and then blindly entered a sell order as per the simple news trade, this particular trade would have been a loser. Had we followed the simple news trade setup as I presented it (that is to say, using 15 minute bars), the trade would have been a winner, but the profit would have been smaller. The entry would have taken place two full bars after the news bar (as indicated by the arrow above), by which time half the move was already over. So this time, the straddle trade got us more profit with a lower risk.

To exit this trade, a trailing stop loss is a good choice, as with the simple news trade. In these news based setups we are looking to take a quick profit from short lived excitement around a news release. As we've seen from the examples so far, the moves caused by news tend to carry through quickly, then the price drifts or reverses. News does not often bring about a new long term trend. We want to be in and out grabbing as much of that initial move as we can, and a trailing stop order is a great way to do that. In this example, depending on how close to the price we trailed the stop order, we probably would have been stopped out in the bar labelled 1 on the chart. If we take the close price of that bar as our exit, we would have netted around 40 pips profit in about 20 minutes. Depending on the size we traded, those 40 pips would be worth anywhere from $40 to $4000, which isn't bad for such a quick trade. The risk on this trade was about 5 pips.

If we wanted to be more aggressive and try and let the trade run on further, a good exit would have been the bar labelled number 2. It ran a long way then retraced more than half the move it had made, a clear sign that the price rise was running out of steam. Another option would have been to wait for three consecutive bars against us, which would have seen us exit at the end of the bar labelled number 3. In this example, all three exits were are a similar level, within about 5 pips of each other.

Here's another example:

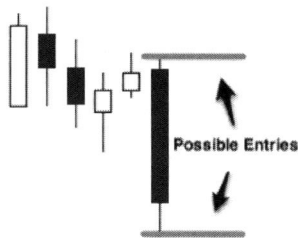

The last bar is the news bar. As it completes, we place a stop buy order at the high of that bar, and a stop sell at the low. Here's what happened next:

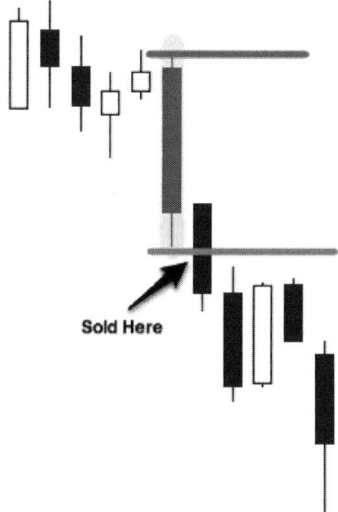

This time the price carried on downwards, so it was the stop sell order that was hit, taking us short. The stop buy order above the news bar remains in place and is now our stop loss, ready to exit the trade if things turn against us. In this case it wasn't required though, the trade followed through nicely, producing a good profit. Here's one last example:

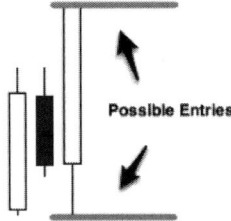

Once again we have a news bar, and we place a stop buy above and a stop sell below. Here's how this setup panned out:

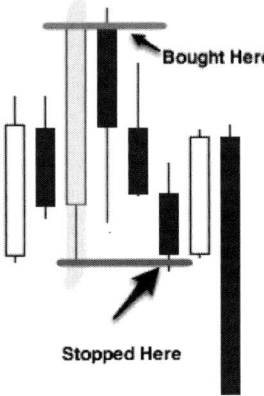

The price initially rose, hitting the stop buy order and thus taking us long. However, it wasn't to be, and it quickly fell back, hitting the stop sell order at the low of the news bar, exiting the trade for a loss.

Make It Your Own

There's really very little to tweak in this setup. 5 minute bars are about the shortest that are viable, any shorter and the initial reaction to the news is still being traded in and the price is too volatile. In making this trade your own, the area to really focus on is the exit. I believe a trailing stop is the simplest and most stress-free option, but you may prefer to try and squeeze every last pip out of the trade by more actively managing the exit, in which case reading and interpreting the price is the way to go.

Setup Number 6: CCI Divergence

We looked a little at divergence when we covered indicators. It's such a powerful signal of a trend change that it is well worth using as a trade setup. Let's remind ourselves of what CCI divergence looks like in action:

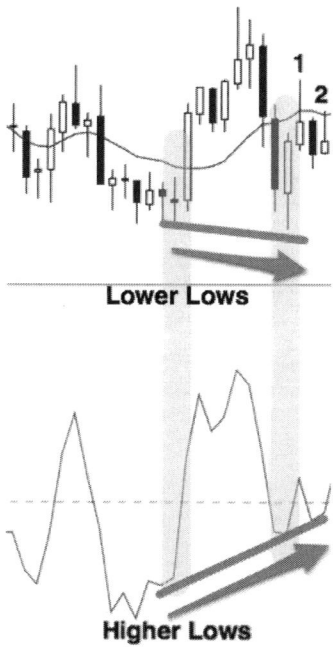

There's quite a bit going on here, more than in previous chart segments, but it's pretty straightforward if we break it down. In the top half of the chart is the price, with a 10 period simple moving average overlaid. The bottom half shows the CCI indicator, set to its default value of 14 periods. The dotted line under the CCI is the zero line.

I've highlighted the divergence signal on the chart. We can see that the price has been very gradually falling, before it rises quickly, and falls back just as quickly. In that period it makes a series of two lows, the second a little lower than the first. The CCI indicator rises and falls at the same time as the price, but *its* second low is considerably higher than its first. The higher lows of the CCI are the opposite of the lower lows of the price, and thus we have a clear case of divergence. The higher lows of the CCI are a leading indicator that the price is set to rise, so this chart is saying we should go long.

Having spotted divergence, we need to figure out when to enter our trade. The divergence itself isn't confirmed until the completion of the bar labelled 1. We need that bar to complete to establish the low made by the previous bar (remember a low bar is one whose lowest point is lower than the lowest point of the bars each side, so we need three bars to establish a low). The earliest time we could enter then, is the start of the bar immediately following bar 1. A better option is to wait for the CCI to cross its zero line, which is an indication price is rising. That would see us enter on bar 2 above. If we wanted to be more conservative, we could wait until the moving average starts to trend upwards, or we could wait until the price breaks above its previous high, which is the high of bar 1. This trade is not like the quick in-and-out news trades, the setup takes an hour or two to complete, and we're looking at the trade itself lasting a similar time. We can afford to get some form of confirmation that the price is indeed starting to rise before we jump in. The CCI zero line cross or the break of the previous high are both good signals in that respect. Let's have a look at what happened next on this chart:

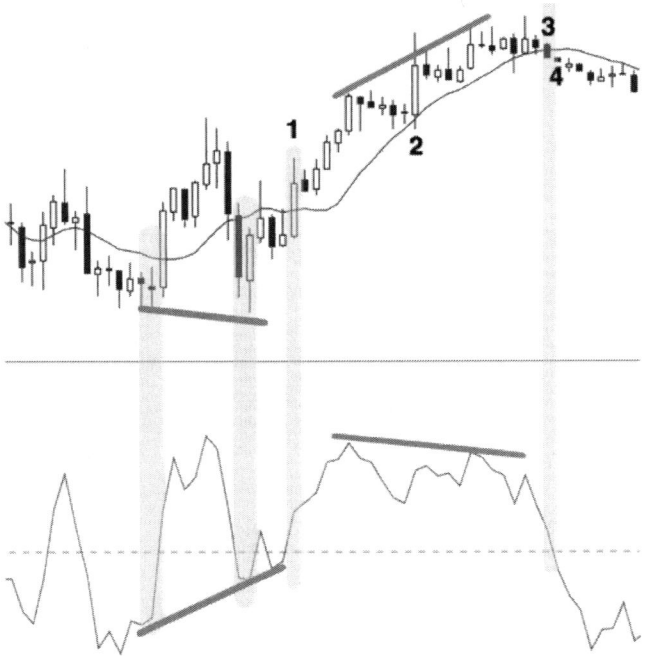

As it happens, the price broke above its previous high and the CCI crossed the zero line all on the same bar (number 1). That would make a great entry point. Once we'd bought we would need to put in our stop loss order. Because our entry is based on a larger pattern and not just two or three bars like previous setups, we cannot automatically pick any particular bar behind which to place our stop. But we can use some common sense. We know we need to keep our losses small, and we also know we need to leave the price some wiggle room because it rarely moves smoothly. There is no obvious support line on the chart behind which we can put out stop, so we just have to use an arbitrary placement. Somewhere between 5 and 10 pips from our entry price is ample. Alternatively we could place it just below the moving average.

We can see from the chart that the price followed through nicely, rising for several bars before dropping back a little, bouncing off the SMA line, then rising a bit more, bouncing, rising, and so on until it ran out of steam. We had a number of exit opportunities here. The first and most conservative was to exit as soon as the price crossed the moving average (number 2). If were willing to take more risk, we could wait until the price closed below the moving average, which happened on the bar labelled number 3. Another exit method is to wait until we see three consecutive bars against us, which happened on bar number 4. Finally, we could have waited for the CCI to drop back below its zero line, signalling the end of the price rise. This also happened on bar number 4. The latest we would want to exit would be that bar, the combination of the CCI dropping back below zero and the three bars against us was a clear signal that the move was over and it was time to take our profit and run.

Something else we can see on this chart is that there was another occurrence of CCI divergence, this time in the opposite direction. The price makes some higher highs, but the CCI makes a series of lower highs, suggesting an imminent fall. This was another clear sign that if we were still in the trade we should really be getting ready to exit. Here's an example of CCI divergence pointing the way to a short trade:

This time the price is making a series of higher highs as it trends upwards, but at the same time the CCI below is making lower highs. The divergence is quite marked, and as we can see it accurately predicted a precipitous drop in the price.

Make It Your Own

The divergence signal leaves much more room for interpretation than the other setups I have discussed so far. It's not one for the novice trader, but rather something to add to your arsenal once you have a little experience under your belt. The setup doesn't give precise entry points and clear places to put a stop loss order (and therefore does not clearly highlight the maximum risk you are taking). Instead it is a signpost pointing the way to a change in price direction. It simply says *"Hey, the price is going to start going up, you might want to jump on board for the ride!"* It's down to you to decide how and when you make that jump, and for how long you stay aboard. Once you have some experience in trading forex, you will be able to make good judgements about when to enter and exit when you see a divergence signal. It is well worth the effort!

Trade Logging

An essential tool for every trader is their journal. In our journal we make notes about every trade that we take. These notes give us the opportunity to improve our trading like nothing else can. Without them, we are trading blind, we are relying on our memory to tell us what is working and what isn't. In the heat of the moment, when exiting a trade that went bad, it is easy to think *"This setup sucks, it never works, I'm dropping it,"* when in actual fact the problem could be that we're not trading it correctly, or even that it works better than our recent memory is giving it credit for. By keeping a journal we are able to look back regularly and objectively at the trades we have taken, and see clearly what is working, what isn't, and why. We can use this information to zoom-in on setups that perform well for our own personal style. As an added benefit, logging trades by physically writing them down forces us to think about each trade. With customisable trading interfaces and one-click ordering, it can become all too easy to get trigger happy and start buying and selling with no real thought behind what we're doing, just half-baked ideas about where the price might be headed. Knowing we are going to be writing down the trade and reviewing our performance keeps us accountable and forces us to think twice before committing money to the market.

Later when we look in detail at trading mentality and the psychology behind successful trading, we will see just how essential our journal is. For now, let's see what it should include. For each trade that we take, we should note the main details. We're not aiming to write a thesis, and we don't want the activity of logging to get in the way of managing the trade, so we just stick to the basics. The following should be noted:

- Type of setup being traded
- Trade direction (long or short)
- Currency pair
- Date and time of entry and exit

- Price of entry and exit
- Initial stop loss order price
- Number of pips profit or loss
- Reason for exiting
- Trade rating (more on this shortly)
- Comments

We can use abbreviations for these details, provided of course that we will be able to understand them later. In our trading plan we can give each setup we wish to use a code. For example, we might call the simple news trade setup "news1", and the news straddle setup "news2". When we start each trading day, we note the date at the top of the page so we don't need to write it down for every trade. A journal entry for a trade can be as short as this:

```
News1 L, GBPUSD, IN 09:45 @ 1.6105
OUT 10:10 @ 1.6155, +50, MA Cross, 4/5 (exited too late)
```

Not too much to write down, just one quick line on entry, and a second quick line on exit. From this we can look back any time and see that we took a news1 trade setup (News1) going long (L) on the GBP/USD pair. Our entry (IN) was at 9:45 and was at 1.6105. We exited (OUT) at 10:10 for 1.6155 because the price crossed the moving average. We made a profit of 50 pips (+50). We rated our execution of the trade four out of five, and believe we exited a bit late.

Wait, what? What's this trade rating? It's a score we give ourselves for how well we think we executed the trade. Our primary job is to execute trades to the best of our ability. Some of those trades will make a loss, and that's quite normal. If we want to keep track of how well we are performing, the profit or loss figure isn't going to cut it. We could execute a trade perfectly and make a 10 pip loss, then execute another trade quite badly, and luck in to a 15 pip profit. Unless we score our execution, we may well look back and think we're doing better or worse than we really are. A simple score out of five is sufficient. A perfect five is awarded when we believe we did everything we should have done. Any mistakes such as jumping in a a bit too soon, losing our nerve and exiting too quickly, or entering on a setup which isn't quite as well formed as it should be perhaps, and we can start knocking off points. Any time we don't score ourselves five, we make a quick note of the reason why.

Trading Plan

We have all heard the saying *if you fail to plan then you plan to fail*, and that's certainly very true of trading. If we trade based on instinct and gut feelings, we're doing little more than gambling. What sets us apart from those spinning roulette wheels in Vegas is that we can bide our time, stack the odds indecently in our favour, choose our moment, and pounce on a trade with a good idea of just how things are going to pan out. In other words, we trade according to a set plan. Provided we follow it, cutting our losers off at the knees, and running our winners to exhaustion, we will make a profit. Our trading plan then, is an essential tool, a key ingredient in the recipe for our success. Such a plan is more than just a list of trade setups like those found in the previous chapter. A good plan will cover all of the aspects below.

The Market

We know that we are trading currencies, but which pairs specifically? We saw previously that not all currency pairs are created equally. We only have one pair of eyes and a limited attention budget, we cannot possibly keep tabs on every pair out there. Whatever pairs we do decide to follow, we want to stick with them. Remember, each pair is like a dialect of the same language. The more time we spend with it, the better we will be able to read and understand its nuances, its behaviour. So the first thing our trading plan should define is the precise segment of the market—the currency pairs—we will be watching and trading.

Time

Unless there is a very good reason for it, we should avoid changing the time frame (bar size) of our chart while day trading. If we see a setup form on a 10 minute chart, and enter a trade based on that setup, we shouldn't then change to a 20 minute chart. Changing time frame can fundamentally change how we see and interpret the price, more so as we zoom in (decreasing the time value of a bar). Certain trade setups, notably news based trades, may require different time settings from others. Our trading plan should include the time frame for each trade setup.

Our plan should also specify the times we will be trading. Different patterns work better at different times of the day. If we trade a bunch of mornings and find a setup that works really well at that time, we cannot assume it will work equally well late at night. Different traders in different countries are trading at different times. The market might be the same, but the conditions are not. We are trying to becomes specialists in our chosen market, and it's much easier to do that if we are always watching that market during the same hours.

Finally on the subject of time, the trading plan should define "no trade zones", the times when we want to stay out of the market. For example, we might decide to exit any trade 5 minutes before all major news announcements, and not to enter any new trades until at least 15 minutes after such news. Clearly news-based trades will be an exception to such a rule.

Entries And Exits

Of course, our plan should include our guidelines on when to enter and exit trades, which is to say, our chosen trade setups. I've given you a starter-kit of setups, and as you gain experience you will create your own. As we collect new setups, we should review which we will continue to trade. It is tempting to keep as many setups as possible in our plan, so we have something available for every occasion. Tempting, but we don't want to be a Jack of all trades and a master of none. The most successful traders use just a handful of setups. It comes down to specialising again. By trading the same patterns over and over, we get deep experience and insight into how those patterns work. Trading them becomes effortless, and we find we can squeeze more and more profit from them. Two or three good setups are all that is necessary to make very good money day trading forex. By all means start out with more, you need to find what works for you. Review your trading plan every week or two, and look at your trading journal to see what's working for you and what isn't. Remove what isn't, and keep what is. When you have a core set of setups that you know inside out, you might want to try inventing new ones. Take them out for a road test, one at a time. Give them a couple of weeks to prove themselves, then decide if they are keepers or not. If you keep a new setup, consider removing an old one.

Money Management

Money management rules are an essential element of any trading plan. These are what are going to keep us in the game long enough to become profitable, so must not be ignored! Your own rules will be defined by your budget and your goals. Unless either change dramatically, those rules will remain in place. Having them written down in your plan will help you stick to them.

Trading Objectives, Goals and Rewards

Finally, every plan should include a section that reminds us why we are doing this. Although it probably sounds obvious now, down the road on the difficult days after suffering a string of losses (it will happen), it can be all too easy to become despondent and lose sight of why we are subjecting ourselves to such punishment. Laying out our objectives before that happens, while we are still motivated and enthusiastic, will help when those dark days come. Write this part of the plan as if you were sending a letter or postcard to your future self, a self who is getting fed up with trading and who needs a boost. Remind yourself of your primary motivation for trading. Add in some goals and rewards too. Trading, when done correctly, can become repetitive and dull. The profits should be just numbers, and as such are not much motivation in themselves. We need something else, and setting predefined rewards for certain goals can really help. For example, we could have an initial goal to make an average of at least 10 pips per day for a week, and when we achieve this, we spend some of our profit on a weekend away, or a fancy meal out, or a new gadget or gizmo. Whatever floats your boat, put it down as a reward for reaching a suitable goal.

Using The Plan

Having put together our personal trading plan with all of the elements above, it is time to put it to use. The plan isn't there to be put up on a dusty bookshelf (or deeply nested folder on a hard drive) never to be seen again. It's an active tool that should be used daily to help us trade better. Ideally we should read through our trading plan every day, before we open our charts and start our session. We start with the objectives and goals, fixing in our mind why we are doing this. Then we go through the rest of the plan, reminding ourselves of our money management rules, the setups we are looking for, and how we will be trading them. After a few weeks of this we probably won't need to read our plan daily, it should be ingrained in our minds, which is a good thing! But we never get complacent, we make a point of reading through the plan at least once a week. It's a good idea at that stage to read through our trade journal at the same time. In this way we can review our performance against our goals. If we did everything we set out to do, we give ourselves a pat on the back. If not, we'll now be aware of where we deviated from the plan, and so will be able to get ourselves back on track.

A Typical Trading Day

You now know enough to get started trading. We've covered a lot of ground, so let's put it all together into what happens during a typical trading day (or trading session, it doesn't have to be a full day).

First off, we start up our trading computer, and make sure it's in the right state to trade. We want to close down email, Facebook, anything not directly related to the job of trading. If there are other people around, they should be made aware that this is trading time, which means no interruptions please! We want to keep our focus on the market, so it's important to eliminate distractions before getting started.

With the computer warmed up and raring to go, we can open our trading journal and start a new page, with the date at the top. At this point, I highly recommend scanning through the written trading plan. A quick visual reminder of what we're looking for can really help us cut down on substandard trades. Next we head to our two economic calendars. We jot down in our journal any scheduled news releases which will occur during the session we are trading, taking note of what they are, when they are occurring, and the currencies most directly affected. If an audible alarm is available, now is the time to set it up for a few minutes before each major news release. There's no point knowing about them then forgetting! With that done we can repoint our web browser towards our favourite streaming news source, and then load up our trading software. We should have our charts and order ticket windows arranged as we like them already. Now we need to be patient, read the charts and wait for an entry. If we're watching multiple currencies, then we can switch our chart between them. The shortest bars we are likely to trade with are 5 minutes, so we need to look at each currency pair at least every five minutes. When we first open our charts we'll spend a bit of time looking back over what has happened since we last traded. Using the tools available in the software, we can draw on horizontal lines at clear support and resistance areas. These can and should remain on the chart throughout the session. All the time we're looking at the charts we are updating our view of the state of the pair(s) we are watching. Where is the major trend? Are we in a period of consolidation? Or are we in a strong move already? Knowing what state the market is in now gives us our first clue as to what we might be looking for. If we're in a strong trend for example, maybe we can get into it using an inside bar or pin bar continuation pattern. We also want to keep an eye on the areas of support and resistance. As new ones appear, we draw them in on the chart.

If and when a trade setup comes along, we keep that particular currency pair's chart open and stop looking at other pairs. We need our focus on the trade at hand. We make a point of going over the setup to see how well it conforms to a model trade. We don't want to be too keen to enter, we aren't trading just for the sake of it. We need to remain emotionally detached and objective about what we're seeing. If it's not right, or something just doesn't feel right, we stay out. We also glance at the time and at our list of upcoming news. If there is news imminent, or likely within the expected duration of the trade, we need to be very cautious, up to and including giving the trade a miss entirely. If everything lines up, and there's no news about to come out to spoil our day, we can enter. We select the best order type to get us in, and we size our position according to our money management rules, ensuring we cannot lose more than our maximum permitted loss for the day. As soon as our entry order is filled, we need to get a stop loss order in. We should already know the price at which we will place it, from our analysis of the setup. If we have a fixed price target, we can also enter a limit order to exit automatically should that target be hit. Once that's done, we can take 30 seconds to note down the trade entry details in our trade log.

With our stop loss order in place, we are protected from major losses should anything go wrong. If something *does* go wrong and the connection to the broker is lost, we must take immediate action. First we must quickly decide if this is a problem that is going to endure more than a couple of minutes. If it's just a case of rebooting the computer or the router then we're probably okay. Anything else and we need to switch to plan B. We call the broker on the phone, or use a backup connection (smartphone app or secondary internet connection) and close the trade, remembering to cancel the stop loss order and any target limit order as well. It's better to be out and miss out on potential profit than be stuck in and get hit with an unnecessary loss if the price turns against us while we're not connected and cannot do anything about it.

Assuming everything works as it should though, we'll be watching the chart unfold. As soon as the price has moved sufficiently that the trade is in profit by 5 pips or more, we can move our stop loss order to the entry price. Now if things go bad we should be able to exit at or around break even. We keep watching the chart, looking for our exit signal. Depending on the setup, our exit may already be defined (for example, a break of a moving average). Even if that's the case, we should continue to read and interpret the chart. Conditions can change, and we need to be ready to adapt. If we have a target limit order in place, we may move it according to the unfolding situation. We don't want to exit early if the price is giving every indication that it's going to blast through our target and keep on going. If the chart gives us a clear indication that it's time to get out, then we get out.

Once we have exited the trade, we must cancel our stop loss order and any target limit order that wasn't hit. We don't want to forget and then find ourselves in an unexpected trade later on because our old stop loss triggered a new trade! Before we move on, we take another 30 seconds to note the exit details down in our trade log, scoring ourselves out of 5 for how well we followed our plan and executed the trade, regardless of whether it made or lost money. Now we're out, we can go back to flipping through our chosen currency pairs, updating our view on what is happening with each, and looking for another possible trade. If we made a loss, we need to decide whether to end our session or not, according to our money management rules and our trading plan rules. If we've hit our maximum loss for the day, we close up shop and don't look back. There will be new opportunities tomorrow.

Once we've exited our last trade, we can go through our charts and clean them up, deleting all the support and resistance lines we drew in at the start of, and throughout the session. This is a great time to add any extra notes to our trade journal. Any observations we may have made about the market, opportunities we spotted but didn't know how to trade (noting these means we'll be reminded to investigate later), and any problems we encountered—technical or market related—that we need to sort out.

Chapter Six

Getting Started

Normally when we learn a new skill, there is a leap of faith somewhere between learning the theory and actually jumping in *doing* it. That leap may be difficult to take financially, particularly if practicing the skill involves spending money on materials. It may also be difficult emotionally, because having a go for the first time is like sitting an exam. We are putting ourselves to the test, and our first time out is going to show up whether or not we actually learnt anything. For us as forex traders, the emotional leap is by far the biggest. We've seen that trading currencies is hardly brain surgery, it's mainly common sense. But if you've never done it, or anything like it before, then it is outside your comfort zone and so needs a mental push to get going. What makes it particularly hard is that your early trades will most likely be disasters. You may get lucky and profit from a few, but by and large you will probably make a loss. When that happens, it's easy to think you're not cut out for it, or that the system must be wrong.

The simple truth is that like any new skill, learning the theory is the first step, the second is hands on practice, repeatedly, doggedly, until it becomes second nature. A few rare geniuses aside, nobody starts out accomplished in their chosen field, it takes work to get there. We'll examine the whole psychological aspect to trading forex in the next chapter, it's very important indeed. For now though, I want to focus more on the practical side of getting started, the steps you need to take and in what order, to go from reading about forex to actually becoming a forex trader.

Your First Forex Account

We are very fortunate these days in that the very first step is easy, and completely free. Your first action is to open a practice, or demo, trading account. There are dozens of these on offer, and new ones seem to pop up every week. There are some suggestions on the Resources page, but typing "demo forex trading account" into your search engine of choice will offer you an abundance of options. Tempting though it may be, I would advise against just picking one at random.

Your demo account isn't just about getting your feet wet and experiencing your first few trades. It is as much about getting to grips with a trading interface—charts and order entry screen. It makes sense then, to learn the ropes using the interface you expect to use when you go live, that is to say, start trading for real. So take a little time to look around and select a broker using the advice offered earlier. Don't get too hung up on this step though. No money is being committed at this stage, and there's no obligation to use the same broker for live trading as for practice, so if you decide you don't like the one you've chosen there's no harm done. Quite the opposite in fact, you will have found out something more about the kind of broker you *do* want to work with.

A word of caution on demo trading accounts. Once you've signed up, you can expect a barrage of emails, phone calls, and letters, all pressing you to take the next step and deposit funds into a live account. You may want to be careful about the telephone number you use when you create your free practice account for this reason!

With your account open, the next step is to get familiar with the software provided for you. Most brokers have very good quick start tutorials and videos, and it is well worth taking the time to watch these. The very best thing though is to simply throw yourself into it and start clicking stuff. Make some trades! Don't worry at first about reading the market and trying to make a profit (even if it's just a demo profit), these early trades are all about seeing how this whole deal works. Don't worry either about losing money. As long as you never provided a credit card number, you are only trading with Monopoly money. These accounts exist as a kind of trading playground, so use them as such. Enter some buy and sell orders. Try basic market orders, see how they affect your (imaginary) balance and available margin. Watch how those change while the trade is open. Try out the different ways of closing trades, by regular orders or by using *Exit* buttons where available. You want to be like a kid in a flight simulator, pushing all the buttons and levers to see what they do. Nobody is going to get hurt and you won't lose any money, it's all good clean harmless fun, and more importantly, experience.

Practice Trading

When you're comfortable with the trading environment, it's time to get a little more serious. If you haven't done so already, you should get your chart set up. You'll need to decide if you want to use bars or candlesticks, and choose a time period. I would suggest 10 minutes or 15 minutes to start out. Add on a 10 period simple moving average. If you've followed the *Missions* in this book, you should be comfortable with these kinds of charts by now, and you'll quickly be able to get them configured in a way that is easy on the eye. What may be new to you is seeing the chart *live*, moving in real time as the prices change. This is your first real chance to see things from the "hard right edge", the developing edge of the chart, as it makes new patterns, sets, tests, and breaks support and resistance levels. Up to now, you've looked at all these patterns after the event, when they are easy to spot. Seeing them form is a whole new ball game. You'll want to spend a good deal of time watching these live charts. Use the drawing tools available to draw on support and resistance levels. Try and pick out major trends, as well as more short term trends. Try and spot patterns as they form but before they complete. And most importantly of all, *trade them*. When you think you've got a signal, buy or sell according to the setup. Once again, don't worry about being right or wrong at this stage. This is a simulation and your goal is to get some practice in a safe environment. We call this kind of practice or simulated trading *paper trading*, because before the advent of nice real time demo accounts, we recorded our practice trades on paper.

You should get into good habits right from the beginning of your paper trading. Start your trading journal, and log all of your practice trades as if they were real. You'll make loads of mistakes to start with, and that's a good thing. Making mistakes now is free. Making them once you are trading live can be very costly indeed! Remember that every mistake should teach you something. Sometimes you'll do something wrong and know immediately what it was. Other times you may need to think about it for a bit before spotting the error. And many times you will do everything right and your practice trade will produce a losing result. That's normal too, and it's as important to get used to these losses as it is to get some practice winners under your belt. Your trade journal is your way of keeping score of your performance. Your execution score should improve over time, and the number of pips won should follow. Combined, these will give you your best indication of when you are ready to take the next step.

Going Live

I am guessing you didn't read this book just to learn how to trade a simulator for the rest of your life. At some point you'll want to turn those paper pips into real results and actual cash. That means making the move from a demo account to a real one. When you do this is entirely up to you. I would strongly advise that you are consistently profitable in your paper trading before you make the change though. Paper trading is much easier than the real thing (there's considerably less psychological pressure), so if you aren't making a profit in a demo account, you can be sure you won't make one in a live account. As the first step in making money is not to lose it, it makes no sense to make that change to live too early and throw real money down the drain. To know when you are ready, you can turn to your trading journal. If you are making a profit more days than you're making a loss, and your profits are larger than your losses, then you are ready.

Depending on your broker, you may well be able to flick a switch in your account settings, add a credit card, and change your practice account to a real one. Other brokers require you to sign up a whole new account for real. It may be that your demo account has shown you that the broker you've been working with is not the one for you. If that's the case, end the relationship and pick a new one. Don't trade live with them immediately though, get a demo account and have a poke around first to make sure your second choice is better than the first, and that you understand and are comfortable with their trading platform.

With your real trading account ready and funded, you can finally start making some live trades. If you have practiced enough then this should be a very simple case of just doing what you have been doing to now, but in your live account. The reality is never quite so simple though. Having real money on the line adds a layer of nerves you won't quite believe at first. Taking those first few live trades can be mentally tough. Just take some deep breaths, and think back to all your practice trading. Take confidence from the results you've seen. You know your trading plan works because you've seen it first hand.

Your first live trades should be taken at the smallest size your broker will let you get away with. The added psychological pressure is much less when going from demo trades to real trades where a 1 pip move is worth 10 cents or less, than trades where every pip move is worth a Dollar or ten Dollars. So start small, very small, and work up. Forex isn't a race, there is plenty of time to make your fortune, no need to risk everything during your first faltering steps. When you are consistently profitable trading very small size, increase it a little. Get used to trading at a Dollar a pip. When you are comfortable there, and still consistently profitable of course, bump things up another notch to two Dollars a pip. I would suggest trading profitably for at least a week at each higher size, and preferably longer. Don't get over confident and try and run before you can walk, you will likely regret it.

Sometimes things won't go well, and you will find that you are no longer consistently profitable. Your losses may become too big or too frequent. Whatever the case, the first thing you should do is scale back your trade size. This runs against your natural instinct which will be to *increase* size to try and win back your losses more quickly. That's just gambling, and is reckless. If you aren't making money there is a reason, and it's important to understand it before risking even more money in the market. Usually the reason comes down to the emotional pressures. Just reducing trade size can often be enough to alleviate these and get things back on track. If it doesn't, at least by reducing your size you will be losing less. You should continue to reduce your trade size until you become profitable again. If necessary you should reduce right back to zero, which means returning to the demo account and not risking any more real money. Taking a break from trading for a few days can also work wonders.

Chapter Seven

Trading Mentality

It is an unfortunate fact that the vast majority of people who try trading forex, fail. Nobody knows the exact numbers, figures from 80% to 95% are regularly bandied about, but nobody is arguing that well over half of all people who have a go at this, are not consistently profitable. That may sound ridiculous, after all, trading isn't that hard is it? You've got this far, you understand how to read price charts and they're pretty straightforward. Spotting patterns or trade setups looks like child's play. All you have to do is watch the chart, enter when the pattern says so, and exit when the right signal comes along. If the trade is a loss, exit quickly. If it is profitable, run it to the maximum. Simple, right?

Well, yes, in as much as giving up smoking is simple. After all, to give up smoking you just don't smoke any more cigarettes. Nothing could be easier, right? Or what about losing weight? That's easy too, all you have to do is eat fewer fatty foods, and do more exercise. It's a super easy two step plan, can't go wrong! And yet, as anyone who has given up smoking, been on a diet, or given up any other vice can attest, knowing what to do is one thing, doing it is quite another.

Trading is the same. It looks easy from the outside. You read the book, learn the steps, then all you need to do is implement them. That's when the hard work really starts. That's when you need to dig deep and find discipline, a cast iron will, and determination like you've never needed before.

No doubt you are reading this thinking *"This doesn't apply to me. I'm determined to do well at this! I'm going to be the exception that proves the rule! I'm not like those other traders who can't stick at it! It's really not that hard!"* And that's okay, everyone thinks that. Yet statistically, you are likely to fail at forex day trading.

I say this not to put you off even trying, far from it. But it's important to be aware of the difficulties that lie ahead before starting this journey. The better you know the obstacles before you, the better equipped you will be to deal with them. Your enthusiasm and determination to not be lumped in with that big majority of losers are great assets, and you'll need every ounce you can muster. The rewards are worth it. But make no mistake, this isn't some hurdle you have to overcome once and then you've made it. These are challenges that you will face every single time you trade, for as long as you continue to trade. Yes, they'll get easier to beat as you gain experience, and confidence. But the moment you let your guard down, the second you say *"I've done it, I've succeeded, I'm good at this"*, that's when you become most vulnerable. That's when the market can turn around and bite your head off.

Hardwired To Fail

Okay, pep talk over, you've got the picture, it's tough to succeed. The question is why? What makes trading so difficult? The answer lies in human evolution, the way our brains are wired. The bad news is, they're wired in a way that sets us up to fail.

Trading correctly requires us to do things that our brains are going to try and stop us doing. Millions of years of evolution have literally programmed us for survival. This is a good thing if you find yourself in a jungle with a tiger approaching. But I'm guessing you don't live in a jungle, and the last tiger you saw was safely behind bars in a zoo. Evolution is slow, and it hasn't caught up with the financial markets. Something as simple as taking a losing trade is going to present you with some difficulties, because evolution doesn't want you to lose.

Loss Aversion

We've seen already how losing trades are part of the business of trading. Indeed we can expect half or more of our trades to be losers, but still make money over all, *provided* that we keep those losses small. When we enter a trade and it doesn't go our way, we need to exit quickly with as small a loss as possible. That requires a physical action. We need to click a button labelled buy or sell, which will instruct our computer to send an order which will take us out of the trade and will remove money from our account. Your conscious mind knows this to be true, and knows you must click that button. But in the heat of the moment, in the trade, with real money at play, something weird happens. A little voice in your head says *"Don't press the button yet, wait a couple of seconds, the price might turn around and come back! Don't take a loss when this could still turn into a win!"* And so you wait, and the loss gets bigger. Your conscious mind knows that you should really click that button now, because things are going from bad to worse. But the little voice hasn't gone away. It's still there, whispering to you *"Hang on, just a bit longer. This loss is big now, it's going to be harder to recover from this. Better to wait and see it turn round. After all, it can't keep going against me forever! It has to go back up sooner or later"*. The button remains stubbornly un-clicked.

Sometimes, the price will come back your way a little. Now you *really* need to click that order button that will exit the trade, after all, you've just been given a temporary reprieve. But no, the voice is still there, and now it's saying *"See! I was right, it's turned round! Wait a bit longer and it will make up all the loss. Another few seconds and I can exit at break even!"* Inevitably, the price goes back against you and before you know it you're sitting on an even bigger loss. The voice says *"Okay, next time the price goes up a bit, I'll get straight out..."* and so the game goes on.

What is this voice with strange power over you? Are you going insane? You know what you should do, yet seem incapable of actually performing the tiny insignificant action of clicking a mouse on a button, one click that will end the misery. The voice is your subconscious mind. The phenomenon is called *loss aversion*, and believe it or not, it's trying to be helpful.

The All Powerful Subconscious

Experts in neuroscience agree that the subconscious mind controls the vast majority of everything that goes on in our brain. Estimates of exactly how much vary, and nobody really knows for sure, but it's probably more than 90%. Some of that stuff is background business like breathing, pumping blood, sending out armies of antibodies to fight off germs or infection, basic housekeeping for the body. But an awful lot of it, more than most of us imagine, is controlling almost everything else we do as well. Even when we think we're in control, more often than not, we aren't. We are actually running on autopilot.

This is a good thing. If we had to consciously think about everything going on around us at all times, and make considered decisions based on all these inputs, we would probably go mad within seconds. There's just too much information there. Take a minute now to stop reading this, and look around you—really look. There is so much *stuff* around you, of different materials, textures, colours. Some of it is inanimate, some might be alive (other people, animals, insects). And that's just dealing with one sense—sight. You've also got sound to process. While reading this book you are probably not paying any attention to the sounds going on around, but if you stop to listen, even in an apparently quiet place, there are all sorts of noises. And smell, touch, and taste are all shovelling data into your brain as well.

All that data is too much to process, so your brain has evolved a system of filters and shortcuts. Most stuff simply gets sifted out straight away, things like sounds while you're reading. But if someone called out your name now, your sound filter would let that through and your attention would instantly be drawn to the person calling you. The same would happen if you heard a scream, or some other sound that indicated possible danger. The other senses also have automatic bypasses to their filters. In the background, your brain is filtering out most of what you see, taste, touch, and smell. If something important looking comes along, it gets through.

Filters are only half the story. The data that does get through is still considerable in quantity. Evolution has once again solved this problem with a clever system of shortcuts. It's wired your brain up with lots of little algorithms, like computer programs, for handling the information that comes in. These algorithms take predetermined actions which, most of the time, result in a good outcome for you without you having to spend time and energy thinking. Brains are lazy and don't like to expend energy thinking, so we rely heavily on these actions. For example, when you're out looking for somewhere to eat and you see three restaurants next to each other on the street, one is very busy, one has a few customers, and one is empty, which do you choose?

Chances are you will be drawn strongly to the busiest one. Your brain is using a well worn shortcut which says *"If everyone else is eating there, it must be good."* Job done, no decision to make, your conscious mind gets away without having to think, and can go back to sleep. This particular shortcut is called *social proof*, also often referred to as the bandwagon effect. When we see lots of other people doing something, we jump onboard. It's the basis for the entire fashion industry, and it's also how a lot of marketing works.

It is easy to see how such a mental shortcut has evolved. When Mr Caveman was foraging in the forest for something to eat, he didn't know which berries or mushrooms were safe, and which were going to make him ill, or even kill him. So if he saw a crowd of other cavemen eating a certain fruit or berry, and doing so without any apparent ill effects, he knew he was pretty safe to eat the same thing. This shortcut is potentially a life saver.

We've already seen how social proof affects us in trading, it is the basis for the self-fulfilling prophecy that plays such a large part in chart patterns working the way they do. Social proof is just one example of what we call *cognitive bias*. It's one of a large number of hardwired shortcuts the brain uses to save us from having to consciously make decisions. When it comes to trading, it's actually pretty handy. But there are lots of other biases which are actively working against us, setting us up for failure before we even switch on the PC.

Cognitive Bias

Our subconscious is an expert at doing what's necessary to keep us alive, and most cognitive biases can be explained by this. Staying alive generally involves things like avoiding danger, keeping warm, and obtaining food. When Mr Caveman went out hunting, his brain was going to give him all the help it could. So when he found a tasty rabbit, and that rabbit decided it was going to do a runner, what was Mr Caveman's brain going to do? It could either say *"That's fine, I'll eat tomorrow"*, or it could say *"Get after that fluffy bundle of meat, I'm hungry!"* I'm sure you can guess which instinct was stronger. The few cavemen without the sense to go after the rabbit, well they didn't get to eat. Carry on like that and it's only going to end one way! Evolution saw to it that those with the instinct to chase were those who survived. Mr Caveman's mind evolved to *avoid loss*, after all, who knows when the next meal might hop by?

This loss aversion instinct to chase after a meal kept Mr Caveman alive, long enough for him to meet a girl, get married, have some baby cave children, and continue the evolution of the human race, which ultimately led to the likes of you and me wandering around. We have the luxury of supermarkets and home delivery, so we don't generally need to go chasing rabbits to eat. But all that programming is still there, deeply embedded in our minds, physically hardwired into the structure of our brains. So when we enter a trade and that trade turns bad, it should be no surprise that our subconscious mind, that part of the mind which occupies and controls 90% or more of our brain, puts the brakes on when our finger reaches for the buy or sell button which will effectively abandon this particular hunt. It says *"No! I'm hungry, I need to chase this trade, don't let it get away!"* Sadly, it hasn't yet figured out that unlike rabbits, there are always more trades just around the corner. It doesn't know about the damage to our account balance that this pointless chase is going to inflict.

The good news is that now we know how our brains are working against us, we can come up with a plan to overcome the problem, and we'll do that shortly. The bad news is that this natural instinct for avoiding loss is not the only hard wired program we have to beat.

Optimism Bias

The brain has another trick up its sleeve. It is called *optimism bias*, and put very simply it means we are overconfident. As you read this, your mind is trying to reject everything I'm telling you about how hard it is to trade profitably. Even with that last sentence, your brain is right now pushing it to one side with a sigh and a *"Nah, this doesn't apply to me, I'm different."* But you're not, and if you had that thought or anything like it, it just goes to prove the point.

Optimism bias is a relatively recent discovery. There's a well known experiment that demonstrates it nicely. In this experiment a test subject is asked to rate the chances of a series of things happening to them. For example, they might be asked *"How likely do you think it is that you will contract cancer in your lifetime?"* The subject responds with a percentage, perhaps they think they have a 10% chance. They are then given the actual answer based on statistical data. In the case of getting cancer, the chance is actually 30%. Then they're asked another question, and the process goes on. So far so simple. Here's where it gets interesting. Once the subject has answered all of the questions, they then get asked them all a second time. This time round they know all the correct answers. So when the question about cancer comes up, they should answer 30%, because five minutes ago they were told that this is the actual risk of them contracting the disease. And yet in almost every case, if the subject had previously underestimated the risk, they give the same answer they gave before.

If they had overestimated the answer the first time round, for example, if they thought their risk of cancer was 50%, then the second time they are asked the question they modify their answer and give the actual, lower, figure.

This experiment clearly demonstrates the tendency for people to accept positive information—that which is deemed beneficial—and to reject negative information. There are all sorts of other studies which demonstrate the same phenomenon. For example, surveys show that newlyweds consistently predict their marriages to last their lifetime, even when they are shown divorce statistics which suggest that is not likely to happen. University graduates underestimate the time it will take them to get a job and overestimate their likely starting salary. Even the pessimists among us are, deep down, irrationally optimistic.

Why does the brain do this? Why do we persistently fail to update our beliefs when negative information is available, but apply positive information without difficulty? It all goes back to Mr Caveman and his fight for survival again. If, after giving chase to the rabbit he was so intent on not losing, the rabbit did eventually get away, Mr Caveman has new information: rabbits can escape. Rabbits, being rapid little blighters, probably escape more often than they get caught. If Mr Caveman updated his belief about his own ability to catch a rabbit every single time he failed to do so, he would soon come to the conclusion that his chances of catching rabbits were very low indeed. So low in fact, that it would appear futile to even try. Such a belief would lead to a very hungry caveman, and weakened from hunger he would be even less successful in his hunting, adding weight to his now overwhelmingly negative outlook on his ability to catch dinner. You can see where this is going. Evolution has seen to it that no matter how many setbacks Mr Caveman encounters in his daily chase, he manages to maintain the belief he will be successful. And with good reason, even if he only gets one rabbit in ten, that's probably enough to live on.

Back in the present, and it should be obvious the problems that optimism bias presents us as traders. We *should* be pessimistic about every trade. We should enter a trade expecting it to fail, so we're better prepared if it does. But our optimistic subconscious is willing us to believe it's going to succeed. Before we enter, it's busily ignoring the signs for caution, and over-emphasising the signals for entry. It's screaming at us *"This is a good trade, take it!"* even if in reality it's a half-baked setup with an average (or worse) chance of success.

In a losing trade, optimism bias is willing us to stay in. Although our eyes see the signals on the chart that say this trade is not working out, our mind—the 90% which is really in control—is blind to those signals. It simply filters them out. *"Everything's fine!"* it says. *"Keep calm and carry on!"* And once again, the finger hovering over the Exit button, remains hovering.

Loss aversion and optimism bias are already formidable opponents to our success, but there are more! In fact, there are a whole raft of additional cognitive biases that we've evolved as shortcuts to an easy life, but which are barriers to profitable trading. I'm not going to dwell on each and every one of them, as by now you should be getting the picture. But it is most certainly worth knowing about them, because that knowledge will help us combat them.

Confirmation Bias

Closely related to optimism bias, confirmation bias works even more actively against us. With optimism bias, we subconsciously reject information which suggests bad things are going to happen. It's like putting our fingers in our ears and shouting *"La la la, I'm not listening to this!"* Confirmation bias on the other hand, sees us actively seek out information that supports our point of view. We love to be right, so anything that strengthens our opinion is attractive to us.

In trading, this means that as we look at a potential setup, we have a natural tendency to look specifically for signals that support an entry, and to over blow them. If we are thinking of going long, the slightest sign of prices rising will be magnified in our minds as a powerful up trend. The most modest increase in volume will be taken as a sign that the whole world is jumping on board. Random candlestick patterns will magically transform themselves before our very eyes to become entry signals so obvious any idiot must surely be able to see them.

Contrast Bias

Picture two cars parked up next to each other, both for sale. One is a second hand Ford Pickup, and the asking price is $20,000. The other is a Maserati Grand Tourismo for $125,000. Looking at these two cars, the Maserati looks pretty expensive, right? But what if instead of the pickup, it was parked next to a Ferrari 458 for $230,000? Suddenly the Maserati looks like a bit of a bargain.

This tendency to measure something in relation to something similar which is close by, either spatially or temporally, is called contrast bias. It's another product of evolution. When Mr Caveman is sizing up a rabbit and a hare as possible dinner, it's easy to compare the relative advantages of each as they nibble the grass side by side. To consider them against other possible meals (maybe a deer, or a wild boar) requires greater mental effort. It means conjuring up an idea of something not actually present. The hare might be smaller than a deer, but the deer isn't around so the hare looks pretty good when compared to the immediate alternative, the little rabbit.

Contrast bias can make the average appear positively marvellous if it's placed next to something awful. By the same token, something good may lose its lustre when viewed in the proximity of something quite astounding.

This once again presents a problem when it comes to trading. A lot of our time as traders is spent sitting watching charts, waiting for a good high probability low risk setup to come along. Until it does, we're most likely watching charts that are going sideways, or jumping around all over the place. After an hour or two of this, the most feeble of potential setups can look rather appealing. If we saw such a setup after having taken a few genuinely great trades, we would likely dismiss it as not being up to par. But in the absence of a quality trade for immediate comparison, we hardly think twice. And of course, our old friends optimism and confirmation bias are both there to coax us into taking that trade. We never stood a chance.

Hyperbolic Discounting

We have a strange tendency to favour relatively small short term gains over much larger long term ones. Given a choice of being given $250 today, or $500 in 12 months, most of us will take the $250. This preference for the short term win is due to *hyperbolic discounting*, so named because subconsciously we discount the value of a future reward, and we do so increasingly, proportional to the delay between now and obtaining it. To put that another way, the further away the reward, the more we discount its value. If we have the choice of being given $250 in ten years, or $500 in eleven years, most people will opt for the $500, after all, it's 100% extra profit for just 10% more waiting time. Yet the delay between the two amounts is a year, exactly the same delay as in the first example.

When it comes to trading, the problem is obvious. As soon as we find ourselves in a winning trade, our hardwired instinct is to exit with some profit at the earliest opportunity. We don't want to risk losing what we've made so far (*loss aversion*), and we're willing to sacrifice the potentially greater profit available if we stay in. The longer we think we need to stay in the trade, the less value we place on the potential future profit. An extra hour staying in to win another $100 profit on top of the $100 we made in the first ten minutes of the trade simply doesn't seem worth the effort and the risk. We'd rather take the $100 we've got, and start looking for the next quick win. It's the exact opposite of what we need to do in order to succeed long term as traders. We *know* we need to run winning trades as long as possible to extract the maximum profit. It's logical, and our brain is perfectly okay with that fact as we sit here and think about it happening some time in the future. But once we're actually in a winning trade, we're much higher up the hyperbolic curve. We've got profit *right now*, and the potential extra profit *seems* a long way off. Subconsciously we discount its value massively. It just doesn't seem worth the risk.

Illusory Correlation

Formula One racing driver David Coulthard has often spoken of his lucky underpants. Given to him by his Aunt, he won his first few karting races while wearing them. Convinced of their ability to bring luck, he continued wearing them for every Formula One race until a particularly bad crash rendered them unwearable. Even after the crash, he continued to bring them to races. Did these underpants have magical abilities? Of course not. Mr Coulthard was simply a slave to *illusory correlation*. His mind made a link between his Aunt's gift and his karting win. Subsequent wins only served to reinforce this correlation between pants and racing performance (and of course, optimism bias neatly filtered out all those races where he wore the pants but didn't win).

For us as traders, we need to take care not to attribute the outcomes of trades to random unrelated circumstances. Noting that a particular trade works better between 10am and midday is good, there's sound reason why that could be the case. Noting that a trade works well when it's raining, or when listening to a certain piece of music, or when wearing certain underpants, is a clear case of illusory correlation.

Outcome Bias

Closely related to both illusory correlation and confirmation bias, is *outcome bias*. This is our tendency to judge our decisions based on their outcome instead of on the quality of the decision itself. If we enter a trade that we know is substandard, but by chance that trade ends up profitable, we are prone to modify our view of the entry we took, rating it as good instead of poor. We congratulate ourselves, instead of reprimanding ourselves. The danger is that next time such a substandard setup comes along, we will be much more inclined to take it, even though in reality nothing has changed. There is no higher chance of the trade being profitable than there was before. A substandard setup is still substandard.

Irrational Escalation

We probably all know someone who spotted an amazing bargain on eBay, got into a bidding war, and ended up paying well over the odds for their lot—more even than they would have paid for a new item from the store. This is *irrational escalation* at work.

Another close relation of confirmation bias and of loss aversion, irrational escalation sees us back up our decisions with actions that are not proportional to the reward. Our need to see our decision through, to be proved right, to *win*, causes us to lose touch with logic.

Paying over the odds on eBay is one thing. Doubling up on losing trades is another. We take a trade, convinced it will be a winner (optimism bias), but it doesn't work out the way we expected. Rather than accept the loss and move on, we fight for what we believe is rightfully ours. We increase the risk on the next trade, maybe double up on the size. We are determined to get our money back. This rarely ends well.

Gambler's Fallacy

Take an evenly weighted coin and toss it ten times. Every time it turns up heads. What are the odds of the eleventh toss turning up tails? The answer is 50:50. If you think that there is a higher chance of tails after such a run of heads, then you are afflicted with gambler's fallacy. To believe that the next toss is more likely to be tails is to suggest that the coin has a memory, that it remembers the previous ten tosses, which is clearly ridiculous. Each individual toss has exactly the same chance of turning up heads or tails.

Trading isn't gambling. We have control over the odds and can stack them in our favour. We can also limit our losses and run our profits to come out ahead. But that doesn't mean we don't get hit with this common error of judgement. After suffering a run of losing trades, it's very easy to think *"The next trade must be better!"* Why must it? The market isn't going to reward you for your previous string of losses. It doesn't *know* about those losses. Each trade performs on its own merit.

Overcoming These Problems

If you've read this far and not given up, thinking this is a losing battle, well done! Certainly our own minds are a formidable opponent, and one we must beat anew every time we trade if we want to do so profitably. But beat them we can. Knowing and using techniques to overcome these obstacles is what separates losing traders from winners. In this section we will look at a raft of measures that don't just fight the barriers put up by our minds, they will actually turn them around and make them work for us.

Upside Down Chart

One of the simplest and most effective methods for seeing what's really on a chart, instead of seeing what we want to see, is to flip the chart upside down. You can do this either physically, or mentally. I'd recommend actually physically flipping charts at least until you get the hang of it, because it stops you cheating yourself. Flipping forex charts is really easy, you just load up a chart for the opposite currency pair. There's no need to actually turn your computer upside down! So if you are looking at a chart of the USD/GBP, you would load up a chart for GBP/USD. You're still looking at the same exchange rate, but the other way round. Now with the chart the other way round, try evaluating it again. If you had been thinking a long looked like a good trade, flip the chart and see if a short looks good. If the upside down chart looks like a great long, you know your original idea was bad. The same thing applies when you are already in a trade, more so even. If a trade isn't working out but you find you are telling yourself it's going to be alright, the price will turn back your way, flip the chart and have another look. Does it look more encouraging like that? If it does, you know you've got a problem.

This technique might sound a little odd, but it's very effective because it hijacks our inbuilt confirmation bias and lets us use its power for good. If we took a long and the price didn't follow through, confirmation bias can blind us to the signs that the trade is going bad. We are blinkered to look for a signal that the price is rising. If we flip the chart and see *more* signals that the price is rising than before, our confirmation bias has just been tricked into proving to us that the right way up, the trade is bad. We have no more excuses and can exit quickly.

Model Pattern Catalogue

In an earlier chapter I talked about the importance of keeping a trading plan. In that plan it is good practise to keep a set of perfect trade examples for each trade setup. When you first start trading you won't have any such examples of course, but your paper trading efforts will soon yield some excellent chart patterns (even if you don't trade them perfectly first time!) Print these out and put them in your plan.

These model chart patterns will make it possible to have your inbuilt contrast bias serve you rather than hinder you. When you see a pattern forming, you can compare it to your model. In doing so you will instantly be able to grade the pattern on your screen. Instead of comparing it to all the dross that has come before, you will be comparing it against a known high quality chart. Hopefully the model will simply confirm that you've got a great potential trade in front of you, but sometimes it will show up a substandard chart for what it is.

Magic Mentor

Most of us have had the kind of days where we start the morning full of good intentions. Maybe we are going to clean the house, cut the grass, wash the car, do some work, bake a cake, or perform some other chore. Then the day slips by and before we know it, it's dark outside and we're settled down with a movie and our favourite beverage. The chores we were so sure we would accomplish have been forgotten about. It happens to us all, and most of the time it happens when we have no accountability. If nobody is standing over us making sure we get the car cleaned, it's too easy to keep putting it off in favour of something more interesting. If we have a spouse, or a housemate, or someone we respect asking us *"Did you clean the car yet?"* then we become accountable, and the chances of the job getting done are dramatically increased.

Trading is the same. It's easy to start the trading session with the best intentions in the world. We've read our plan, reviewed our model chart patterns, we know what we're looking for, and we're going to sit patiently until it comes along and then trade it by the book. Unfortunately, those intentions often slip out of the window after some time sat watching sideways charts. We want some action, we want to put some money in our accounts. Substandard patterns start looking more attractive. Maybe we take a peek at a few exotic currency pairs to see if there's something interesting happening elsewhere. Or we switch the timeframe of the chart, trying to spot patterns that just aren't there. If we reach our maximum loss for the day, perhaps we elect to take "just one more trade..." All this deviation from the plan is possible because nobody is watching our backs. There's nobody standing over us, ready to scold us if we do something we shouldn't. We aren't accountable to anyone but ourselves, and it's easy to cheat ourselves.

So what can be done? The best solution is not the easiest: get a mentor. If there is any possibility of getting someone to actually stand over you and make sure you follow the plan, then I recommend doing so. They don't need to be a trader, it can be a friend, family, anyone. What is important is that you have briefed them on your plan. A ten minute overview should be plenty. Tell them *"I'm looking for this chart to make patterns like this or this. When I enter trades it will be for this size. I won't allow myself to lose more than X trades today, or more than Y pips. If you see me do anything other than that, ask me to explain why."* Now when you start trading, you're accountable to your "mentor". If you go off-plan, you are going to have to explain yourself. Of course, you may also have to explain yourself even as you are on plan, but that won't be a problem.

It's not always easy to find someone available and willing to watch you trade all the time. That's why I highly recommend using a *magic mentor*—an imaginary one. Before you dismiss the idea as crazy, hear me out. You're probably thinking that imaginary friends are only for kids, but you'd be wrong. In fact, imaginary mentors have been used by some of the most successful people in history.

Napoleon Hill, the author of the famous *Think and Grow Rich* self help book talked at length in that very book about his invisible counsellors, a group of people from history who he found impressive and wished to imitate. The group included Edison, Darwin, Ford, and Napoleon. He chose them based on certain character traits he wished to acquire. Every evening he would hold an imaginary council meeting with these men, conjuring up images of them in his mind, and imagining himself talking to them. As time went on, the meetings in his head became more and more real. Instead of Hill simply imagining conversations, the men started to speak for themselves, offering words of wisdom and advice. In fact at one point they became so real to him he stopped holding his meetings out of fear that he was going insane, although he later resumed (on the advice of one of his imaginary councillors no less), and even expanded the group.

Hill is by no means the only person to employ imaginary aides, and the method has become mainstream. I'm not suggesting here that you need such a group, but the technique itself can be used very effectively as a replacement for a physical trading mentor, and if used properly can actually be even more powerful than using a friend or family member for the role.

In your mind's eye, you'll need to create an image of your magic mentor. You can make them look however you want, female or male, young or old, it doesn't matter as long as you can imagine yourself having respect for them. In your imagination, you should imbue this mentor with great wisdom. By all means add in some trading knowledge too if it helps. The main thing is that to you, they are someone you respect and can feel accountable to. It's worth spending a bit of time on this. Take fifteen minutes when you can be alone and relaxed, in a quiet place. Close your eyes and build your perfect mentor. The more detail you can add, the better. What are they wearing? What colour is their hair? Are they sitting or standing? How do they speak? Detail adds depth and will make your mentor seem more real. If you can bring up an image your mentor in your mind as easily and clearly as you can a parent or spouse, then they can—and will—seem equally real to you.

Once you've got your mentor fully formed, you need to reinforce their image. Try and spend a few minutes each day picturing them in your mind. Talk to them. You'll have to imagine their responses of course, but that's all part of the process. The more time you can spend getting to know your magic mentor, the more real they will become to you.

Now when you trade, you can have your mentor accompany you. Before you get started, close your eyes for a couple of minutes and bring your mentor centre stage in your mind. Brief them on your trading plan for the session ahead of you. Tell them how you plan to trade, the patterns you are looking for, the maximum loss you are going to take, and so on.

Finally, as you trade, give a running commentary to your mentor. Do this out loud, as if they were actually sat beside you. No, I'm not crazy, I am asking you to talk to an imaginary friend! And with good reason. Doing so will help in two ways. First, vocalising (the process of putting thoughts into spoken words) is one of the single best ways of organising those thoughts. Watching a chart in silence, all sorts of things will cross your mind. Speak them out loud, and you are forced to bring order to them, to consider them individually, and even to justify them. It is one thing to have a fleeting idea that *"This chart looks pretty poor but maybe it's worth a punt"*, and quite another to actually say that out loud. Most of the time, doing so will be enough for you to see how silly some of these ideas are, and you will instantly dismiss them.

The second reason is more subtle. Speaking your thoughts to your mentor will again help to reinforce their image in your mind. The stronger their image, the more you will feel accountable to them. When you take any trading action, be it entering or exiting a trade, or holding position (or lack of position), having to disclose that action to someone you respect will force you to justify it, to explain the reasons behind it. If you are about to enter a trade after having already reached your maximum loss for the day, you will hopefully feel guilty. The more real your mentor seems, the stronger the sense of guilt and the greater chance it has of getting through to you, stopping you from taking an action you know to be wrong.

I know that nine out of ten people who read this chapter will likely dismiss it as kids stuff, or as madness. But the one out of ten who actually tries it and sticks with it is the one who is going to go on and succeed in trading, whipping those other 90%. To be extraordinary in any endeavour takes an extraordinary effort. It requires you to step out of your comfort zone and try something different. Doing the same old thing just renders the same old results. The magic mentor is a hugely powerful tool, and so I urge you to use it.

The Golden Ticket

A large proportion of trading discipline problems manifest themselves the same way—as over trading. Taking trades after the maximum loss has been reached, or the profit target for the day has been attained; entering substandard trades; trading too close to news; trading outside of predefined times, or trading pairs which are not on the plan. These are all examples of over trading, and it's a problem that afflicts all traders at some time in their career. New traders are particularly at risk. Lack of experience, over confidence, and a strong desire to get stuck in and make trades all combine to encourage the novice to jump in without due consideration. Sometimes these ill-thought out trades will work out, more due to chance than judgement, and confirmation bias and illusory correlation will fill the trader with erroneous ideas about what works.

Having watched traders (new and old) make these mistakes time and again over many years, I have found that by far the most effective technique for combatting the problem is what I call the *golden ticket* method. It is as simple as it is potent. On a given day, the trader sets themselves a hard limit of a single trade. That's it, just one trade. Once that trade has been taken, whether it's a winner or a loser, the broker software is closed. No more trades until tomorrow. The golden ticket is a one-shot deal.

The reason this works is because it forces you to really think about every aspect of a trade before pulling the trigger. When we know we only have one attempt at some-thing, we will give it our very best effort. My brother loves to play Mario games on his Wii. He jumps around all over the place, exploring these strange worlds, testing out bizarre objects and hidden rooms. At the start of each game he's pretty carefree, he'll jump on or into anything. Invariably this results in him getting "killed", repeat-edly. When he gets down to his last life, his tactics change dramatically. Suddenly it is his last chance to beat his high score. One false move and he has to start over. He plays with caution, even a degree of thought!

Having one "life" when trading has the same effect. As you look at a chart setting up you will have to consider whether it really is a great pattern, or is it actually quite mediocre and you're just looking for action. You will examine every aspect of the chart with clarity of thought and purpose. And once in a trade, you will feel compelled to manage it to the absolute best of your ability. You are spending your golden ticket for the day, and you want to spend it wisely, getting the most value from it.

Once the trade is over, close the broker platform. You may wish to keep your charts open and paper trade the rest of the session, there's nothing wrong with that. But commit to not taking another live trade until the next day.

When you believe you are ready, when you are making consistently good decisions and are managing your trades properly, raise your limit to two trades a day. Now you have twice the potential to make a profit each day, but two shots is still enough of a limit to make you pause for thought before pushing that buy or sell button.

Then simply rinse and repeat. When you feel you are ready, increase your limit by another one trade a day. Eventually you may feel you can remove the limit altogether, but actually I recommend you keep some form of restriction in place as part of your plan. It will remind you not to get trigger happy, to value every trade opportunity.

When you hit a bad run (and you will, it is inevitable every now and then), reinstate your trade limit. Maybe drop it to three, and if the problems persist, go right back to one and then make yourself work for a raise.

Pips Not Prizes

We've already looked at loss aversion and how we'll sabotage our own efforts to do the right thing because of our *fear* of losing money. To make life harder, we are also pulled in the other direction by greed, the emotion by which our other cognitive biases manifest themselves. Our desire to increase our account balance plays into the hands of optimism bias, irrational escalation, and all the other enemies of rational thought. It pushes us to take unnecessary risks, or make careless decisions.

To reduce the impact of these two very primal emotions, it is very helpful to try and disassociate the actions of trading from the money that it makes or loses. That's easier said than done, after all, we are in this for the cash. But that doesn't mean we have to focus on that cash while we are working. After all, if you have a day job, I suspect you do that job in order to get paid, and I also suspect that you don't spend every minute of every working day trying to figure out how much you earned since your last coffee break. You do the job to the best of your ability, and know that the cash will arrive at the end of the month.

Trading should be the same. We should commit all of our focus and attention to executing great trades correctly, on doing the job of trading. If we do that, the money will come, and we won't even have to wait until the end of the month to see it. How do we divorce our account balance from our trade execution? After all, the two are intimately linked. We need to know our balance in order to manage our risk. The answer is that we don't need to know our balance every minute of the day. At the start of the session we must ensure that we have funds available to trade with. Assuming we have a proper money management plan, we know the maximum amount we can lose in the session ahead of us if it all goes wrong. If we mentally set that aside as being the cost of trading for the day, if we assume it's lost before we even open a chart, we can already begin to distance ourselves from it.

The next step is to disassociate monetary values from individual trades. Instead of looking at a chart and thinking *"This trade coming up has a profit potential of $50 for a risk of $20 if I place a stop there"*, think in terms of pips. The $50 potential profit becomes 50 pips (at $1 a pip), and the risk is 20 pips. You know full well how much each pip is worth from the size you are trading, but even so, thinking in terms of pips and not Dollars will put a little extra distance between you and the money. Not only that but as you increase your trading size over time, provided you continue to think in terms of pips, you won't add nearly as much stress to your trading. Doubling your size may well make a pip worth $2 where last week it was worth $1, but a pip is still a pip, and provided you continue to think that way, your risk won't have increased at all.

Finally, focus all your efforts on trade execution. You know your potential profit and maximum loss, those are a done deal. You can't make the trade go one way or another, that's out of your control. The only thing you *can* control is yourself, your execution of the trade. It doesn't matter if the trade is profitable or not, what matters is that you follow the plan, that you get the best entry you can, and the best exit you can. If that means exiting with a loss, that is perfectly okay, provided you make it the smallest loss you can. If you do, give yourself a pat on the back! You did a good job and that's what counts. Continue to do a good job every time, and the money will flow into your account.

Logbook

I mentioned earlier the importance of logging trades, and it bears repeating here. For every trade we want to write down our reason for entry and exit. If possible, it is best to write it longhand, using a pen not a keyboard. Writing longhand uses a different part of our brain to typing. It requires more effort and that means we put more thought into what we are writing, which in turn means we are forced to think about the trade we are writing about. In other words, just the act of writing down our reason for the trade will by itself make us focus more on the execution of that trade.

Writing your trades down is only half the story. Reading your logbook provides an even greater opportunity for improvement. You should always put some temporal distance between your trading session and reading back your notes. Ideally, a nights sleep, i.e. read your notes the day after you traded. If you can't do that, then at least wait a few hours, and try and do something completely unrelated to trading between writing and reading your logbook. Doing so will help you approach those notes with a clear head, a fresh pair of eyes. The longer the time between writing and reading, the more critical you will be and the more value you will get from the exercise. If you examine your notes too soon, the reasons for each trade will still be fresh in your memory, and you will still be justifying those reasons to yourself based on that memory of events, rather than based on reality. Look at the notes a day (or even better, a week) later, once the memory has faded, and often you will find it is like reading the notes of a stranger. In the cold light of day, away from the market, away from the stress, and most importantly, away from the emotion, you can read back your notes objectively and with a clear head. You can be, and most likely will be amazed by some of what you wrote. Trades that seemed obvious or great in the heat of the moment, will be seen for what they really were. Decisions that you felt were easily justifiable while you were caught up in the excitement of the session, may appear rash and careless when viewed from the perspective of hindsight. And this is a good thing! Seeing those rash decisions, laying bare poor execution, that is the way we learn. It's how we improve at anything, not just trading. Taking a step back, and asking *"Let's see, how did I do?"* is the only way to spot the mistakes. Once spotted, you can figure out how to avoid making them again in the future. If you notice from your logbook that you are consistently taking entries based on substandard chart patterns, print out your model patterns and stick them up next to your screen. Make it part of your routine to check every entry against them before clicking the buy or sell button. Force yourself to stand up and turn around on the spot twice repeating the words *"I will check this chart against the model before I trade!"* if you have to! Do whatever it takes to break the bad habit and force a new one. If your logbook shows you are overtrading, enforce a golden ticket one-trade-a-day restriction. If you are not running winners to their proper conclusion, try and understand why. Is fear of loss making you lose your nerve? If so, trade down to smaller size, or paper trade, until you have confidence in the pattern to see it through every time. Maybe you will discover that you stay in losing trades too long. You already have a technique to overcome that: flip your charts upside down and see if it changes your opinion of where the price is headed.

Without your logbook, you will find it hard to see these problems. People generally have a better opinion of their ability than the reality. It's normal to *think* we're doing the right thing, to believe we are executing every trade perfectly. Only through objective self observation can we stand back and see what we're really doing. It might not be a pretty sight, but it's better to know the truth and have a go at fixing it than to plough on in blissful ignorance.

Meditation

If there is one "secret of my success" in trading, it has to be regular meditation. There's nothing spiritual or religious here, meditation is simply a way of relaxing. A lot of folks go through life without ever properly relaxing. Stressful day jobs, noisy households, televisions and iPods constantly blaring out sound, it's little wonder why. We are bombarded with stimuli all day every day. It's hard to switch off. Most people I know think that they are relaxing when they settle down in front of the TV, or when they go out with friends. But that isn't true relaxation. To be truly relaxed, you need to remove all stimuli, and that's what meditation does.

Before we look at easy meditation techniques, it is probably a good idea to explain why it is such a useful practice. After all, relaxation and manic financial markets are polar opposites. Regular relaxation is important for two reasons. Firstly, it reduces stress like nothing else can. Sure, there are other ways of dealing with stress. A good game of squash, a long walk, or blasting aliens on a video game are all touted as working, but these activities don't go deep. They help us to forget stress, they don't make it simply evaporate in the way regular meditation does. Meditate daily, and you will feel less stressed *all the time*. That helps enormously when it comes to trading. A relaxed trader makes better decisions. Have you ever had that feeling of being in the zone when working on something? You feel like you have an amazing level of focus and clarity of mind, everything seems to just click into place and seem easy? You get that feeling every day when you meditate regularly!

The second reason I recommend meditation is because it is the most powerful way to take control of yourself. With cast iron discipline we can beat our cognitive biases into submission, but not many people have cast iron discipline. Meditation gives us a direct line to the subconscious mind. We can quite literally reprogram ourselves to be better traders, when we meditate. When we are in a truly relaxed state, our mind opens. We can use that opportunity to poke around inside and retune our controls. We can turn down the loss aversion and the various biases, and turn up the discipline.

I know a lot of people who read this will completely dismiss the idea of meditating. It sounds too new age, too unrelated to trading, or just too odd. Those people will likely fall into the 90% of traders who fail. The fact is meditation is a tool used by professionals the world over, particularly sportsmen and women. All athletes at the top of their game meditate daily, it's simply part of the job. Trading is like sport in many ways, there is a need and desire to win, and a strong fear of losing. Traders and sportsmen both have a small fixed window of opportunity to get their game on, to hit the mark, to perform. If the world's top sportsmen and women are all using meditation, you can bet that it's going to help us traders too.

Meditation is essentially a deep relaxation without external stimuli. There are all sorts of different ways to meditate, and here I will share two simple methods with you. They are both very effective, and either one will serve you well.

Meditation Technique One

If you have never done any kind of mediation before, then I would suggest you start with this exercise. Once you have done this a few times, you can add in the second technique.

Start by finding a comfortable position. Sitting is good, lying down better. Be somewhere you won't be disturbed, and somewhere quiet. Close your eyes, and count down slowly, from 25 to 1. As you count down each number, try and visualise it in your mind's eye, that is, try and picture the number in your imagination. Concentrate on each number, its shape, the outline of the figure. There is no right or wrong speed for doing this, just take your time. Don't rush, but don't take so long that your mind starts to wander between numbers.

When you've finished the countdown, concentrate on your feet. Just put all your mental effort into feeling your feet. Feel them become heavier and heavier, as if they were made of lead. Focus all your thought on those feet. When you feel they cannot become any heavier, move your concentration to the bottom half of your legs. Imagine them becoming heavier and heavier.

Move slowly up your body, repeating the process, your knees, thighs, hips, belly, chest, hands, arms, elbows, shoulders, neck, chin, face, to the top of your head. With each step, stay focussed on that part of your body until it becomes heavy. You might find that as you do this you lose the feeling in your body as you move up—this is good! If that happens it means you are entering a deep state of relaxation.

The whole exercise should take around 30 minutes if done right, although you won't know how long you've taken until you've finished because you will lose all track of time during the process. When you have finished, you should be deeply relaxed. You can bring yourself out of the meditation by counting slowing from 1 to 10. When you reach 10, open your eyes and say (out loud if possible) *"I am wide awake, relaxed, and my mind is clear and focussed!"* You will still be feeling pretty chilled out at this point, and it's a great feeling.

When you try this exercise, don't worry if you break your concentration, after all, it is just an exercise and you'll get better with practice. Also don't worry if you fall asleep the first time you do this— I did! Again, with practice you'll slowly gain control. I'd recommend that to start with you try and do this exercise two or three times a week. You might want to do more as it can become quite addictive, but it's quite a time consuming meditation, so technique two is better for use every day.

Meditation Technique Two

This second exercise is a quicker way of reaching a meditative state, and can be used for shorter periods. It's ideal for use as a five or ten minute relaxer before you start trading each day. Use it daily and you will feel in control of your actions like never before.

As with the previous exercise, you will need to find a comfortable position, away from noise and disturbance. Close your eyes, then bring your hands together so that the tips of all your fingers on one hand touch the tips of all your fingers on the other hand, just finger tips, the palms of your hands don't need to touch. You will keep your hands touching like this throughout the exercise, so you might want to rest the base of you hands on your belly or your legs depending on how you are lying down or sitting. Now count down from 50 to 1. Again, take the time to picture each number in your mind's eye as you go. Focus entirely on each number. Don't think about how much time to spend on each number, just take the time that feels right. By the time you get to 1, you should be very relaxed. If you've been doing the previous exercise, you may well find that you feel you're floating, that you've become detached from your body. If that happens, it's an excellent sign and means you reached a deep level of relaxation. You can remain in that relaxed state for as long as you need. In the next section we'll look at a few things you can do while there. For your first few times though, you'll probably just want to come back out straight away. To do that, count from 1 to 10, and when you reach ten, pull you hands apart and say *"I am wide awake, relaxed, and my mind is clear and focussed!"*

After you have done this exercise three or four times, you can reduce the countdown so instead of starting at 50, you begin at 40. A few more days like that, and then you can count down from 30. Eventually you should be able to reduce the countdown to just 10, as with practice you will be able to reach the relaxed meditative state more quickly and easily. When you are at the stage whereby you can meditate with just a countdown from 10, you can really make the most of the technique, almost any time and any place. With practice, you'll be able to meditate even in noisy environments. Boring commutes, waiting in airport lounges, all these dead times become opportunities to drop into a quick meditation. As well see shortly, these quick sessions can be used for all manner of things.

The touching of your fingers is a useful step to include, because it's a trigger. By touching your fingers together every time you meditate, you make a subconscious association between that action and a deeply relaxed state of mind. The more often you repeat the exercise (with your fingertips touching), the stronger the connection your mind will make. You can then use the association to quickly relax yourself at any time. Just bring the tips of your fingers together like in the meditation. Because your subconscious has this association ingrained, the action will relax your mind instantly. It is a great technique for calming yourself in times of stress. If you're about to enter a trade but are nervous about hitting the button because of natural loss aversion, touch the tips of your fingers together and you'll find that fear drain away. If you're in a winning trade and feel the urge to exit early, to take the profit and run, touch the tips of your fingers together and feel a flood of much needed confidence. The great thing is you can use the technique any time, not just in trading. Meditation gives you tools for life!

Taking It Further

These exercises are both designed to get you to a meditative state, and that alone will help you stay relaxed and focussed. But there is much more you can achieve. While in the relaxed state, there are all sorts of things you can do. As I already alluded to, you can reprogram yourself, it's essentially self hypnosis. Anything you tell yourself while meditating, will go directly into your subconscious, that part of your brain responsible for at least 90% of everything you do. So once in a meditation, use your time there to repeat some affirmations to yourself. These can be anything you want, with a couple of caveats. The first is that you must believe in the affirmation. Telling yourself *"I am always in control of my actions"* or *"I always follow my trading plan"* or *"I trade without fear or greed"* are all fine, but something like *"I am the greatest trader who ever lived"* will get thrown out by your subconscious mind's bullshit filter!

The second caveat is that you should stick to the same wording each time you use an affirmation. Always using *"I never think about money when trading"* is good, but changing it to *"I never think about the Dollars when I trade"* one day and then *"I always think in terms of pips not prizes"* the next is just going to confuse matters. So spend a few minutes to come up with two or three good affirmations you want to use before you meditate, and stick with them. Of course, you can add to them or change them over time, but make sure you stick with them a while because the more you use them, the deeper into your mind they'll go, and the more a part of your personality they will become. This is truly powerful stuff, and again, top sportsmen use these kinds of techniques every day. If they are good enough for Olympic athletes, they are good enough for us.

Relaxation Aides

If you find the exercises difficult, maybe you have trouble focussing or just simply relaxing, then you may want to try relaxation CDs or MP3s. These are often marketed as being made for all sorts of specific purposes like giving up smoking, increasing energy, being happier, etc. It really doesn't matter what kind of CD you use, they are all much the same. As long as they have a repeating sound pattern, usually some form of *binaural beat,* then they will help you to get into a relaxed state. If you do use an audio aid, try to not become reliant on it, keep up with the standalone exercises.

They have the benefit that you can do them anywhere any time, without having to plug in headphones.

MISSION: Put aside half an hour when you know you won't be disturbed, and try meditation technique one. Don't worry about "getting it right", there is no right or wrong. Just have a go, and see how you feel afterwards. If you get any positive effect at all, it will give you an insight into the benefits available from regular practice. Try and use the second technique two or three times a week. If you start today, by the time you come to trade live, you will be mentally stronger and more prepared, and have a much higher chance of success.

Trading Mentality — Summary

You may not need to use all of the techniques discussed in this section all of the time, but it's a good idea to use as many of them as you can as regularly as you can. Make them habit so you do them without thinking about it. Internalize them. Human beings are creatures of habit. We can either choose our habits or let them choose us. By starting out on the right foot, using these methods from the get go, they will become habit and you won't need to consciously think about them. They will become part of you and your way of trading. Do this and you will be ahead of 90% of everyone else out there in the market.

Glossary

Ask Price — The price at which we can buy the quote currency.

Bar — A single element on a price chart, showing the range that the price travelled during a given period of time, as well as the price at the start and end of that period.

Base Currency — The first currency in a forex pair. This is the currency used to purchase the quote currency.

Bid Price — The price at which we can sell the quote currency.

Body — The thick part of a candlestick. The body shows the open and close prices for the period of time covered by the candlestick. A solid body indicates that the open price was higher than the close price. An empty body indicates that the close price was higher than the open.

Breakout — When price breaches a support or resistance line, or trend line.

Broker — An agent through which purchases and sales of stocks, commodities, bonds, futures, or currencies are conducted.

Candlestick — A single element on a price chart, showing the range that the price travelled during a given period of time, as well as the price at the start and end of that period.

Consolidation — When price becomes constrained between a support and resistance lines after a period of trending.

Day Trade — A trade which is entered and exited during the same day.

Down Side — When a breakout occurs due to falling prices, this is said to be a breakout to the down side.

Down Trend — A period during which prices are generally falling. Usually defined as a series of lower highs and lower lows.

Fill — The completion of an order.

Fill Price — The price at which an order is filled.

Forex (FX) — Foreign Exchange, the generic term for the global market in which different currencies are bought and sold.

High — A bar (or candlestick) whose highest point is higher than the highest point of the bars on either side.

Instrument — A tradable product. Currencies, stocks, futures, bonds, and CFDs are all examples of financial instruments.

Interbank Rate — The wholesale exchange rate as being traded between top tier market participants (banks).

Intraday — Any time scale less than one day. 5 minute charts, 30 minute charts, and hourly charts are all examples of intraday charts.

Limit Order — An order to buy or sell at a specified price or better.

Limit Price — The price used in a limit order.

Linear Scale — The most common price scale used on price charts. The vertical distance between prices remains constant. The distance between 1.12 and 1.13 is the same as the distance between 2.23 and 2.24 for example.

Log Scale — See Logarithmic Scale.

Logarithmic Scale — An alternative price scale used on price charts. The vertical distance between prices is proportional to the percentage change in those prices. Therefore the distance between 1.12 and 1.13 on a price chart will be double the distance between 2.23 and 2.24 on the same chart, as the percentage difference between those lower prices is double the percentage difference between the higher prices.

Long — A trade in which a purchase is made with a view to selling later at a higher price to realise a profit.

Low — A bar (or candlestick) whose lowest point is lower than the lowest point of the bars on either side.

Market — A place where goods, services, commodities, or currencies are exchanged. In the case of forex, the market comprises all owners of money participating in the exchange of currency.

Pip — One ten-thousandth of a unit of currency (the fourth decimal place). Usually the smallest amount by which a currency quote can move.

Position — An open trade. If we have bought with a view to selling later, our position is long. If we have sold with a view to buying back later, our position is short. It is possible to hold multiple positions at the same time.

Price — The measure of how much something costs in a given currency.

Quote Currency — The second currency in a forex pair. This is the currency bought with, and sold for, the base currency.

Resistance — A level above which price has failed to rise on at least two subsequent occasions.

Retail Broker — Brokers enabling trades for lower level market participants including the general public, and day traders.

Short — A trade in which a sale is made (by borrowing from the broker) with a view to purchasing later (to reimburse the broker) at a lower price, realising a profit.

Signal — An indication on a chart that suggests a good time to buy or sell.

Slippage — The difference between the price when a market order is sent and the price at which it is filled.

Spread — The difference (in pips) between the bid price and the ask price.

Stop Order — An order to buy or sell at a specified price or worse.

Stop Price — The price specified in a stop order.

Support — A level below which price has failed to fall on at least two subsequent occasions.

Tail — The thin line descending from the bottom of the body of a candlestick. The bottom of the tail shows the lowest price reached during the time period the candlestick is representing.

Trend — A period during which prices are generally rising, or generally falling.

Trend Line — A support or resistance line drawn on a chart, connecting multiple highs or lows.

Triangle — A chart pattern in which price is constrained by either up trend and down trend lines simultaneously, or by an up trend line combined with a resistance line, or by a down trend line combined with a support line.

Up Side — When a breakout occurs due to rising prices, this is said to be a breakout to the up side.

Up Trend — A period during which prices are generally rising. Usually defined as a series of higher highs and higher lows.

Wholesale Broker — A broker who enables transactions between top tier market participants (banks), at the interbank rate, for a relatively small commission. Deals in vast sums of money daily.

Wick — The thin line emanating from the top of the body of a candlestick. The top of the wick shows the highest price reached during the time period the candlestick is representing.

Also By The Author

Learn how to trade the US Stock Market, the world's largest and most liquid equity market. In *How To Day Trade Stocks For Profit*, Harvey Walsh uncovers the techniques and trade setups used by professional NASDAQ day traders.

The book is a complete course designed to get you quickly making money from the stock market. No previous trading experience is necessary. Easy to read and jargon-free, it starts right from the very basics, and builds to a remarkably simple but very powerful profit generating strategy.

Readers of this book make real money. Here's what just a few of them had to say:

"Have been using the info in your book for three days... $1,490.00 in the bank."

"It was a great day! I made a $1175.50 profit."

"Per 1 January I started day trading full time."

"I am already making my job salary in trading."

"I ended my first day of live trading with a net profit of $279.53."

Now in its third major edition, *How To Day Trade Stocks For Profit* has helped countless people go from novice to full time day trader.

You can purchase *How To Day Trade Stocks For Profit* from all good online bookstores. It is available in paperback and in all electronic formats.

Printed in Great Britain
by Amazon.co.uk, Ltd.,
Marston Gate.